Literary editor,
Spenser Lyon

Dark Salt /
Dark Soul

Michael Markevich

authorHOUSE®

AuthorHouse™
1663 Liberty Drive
Bloomington, IN 47403
www.authorhouse.com
Phone: 1 (800) 839-8640

Published by AuthorHouse 12/20/2017

ISBN: 978-1-5462-2124-1 (sc)
ISBN: 978-1-5462-2122-7 (hc)
ISBN: 978-1-5462-2123-4 (e)

Library of Congress Control Number: 2017919060

Print information available on the last page.

Dark Salt / Dark Soul

Point creation - Nuclear furnace - Rational organic

WHAT IS PURPOSE of a star? Is intention of nuclear furnace eventual formation of rational organic? Would a star have any purpose without time line, evolution or motive toward rational organic? As has been recognized in so many ways, the human species is made from star dust.

"Distribution of elements in "life" on Earth resemble composition of stars far more than that of elements of Earth. As a result, "life" elements are more cosmically abundant than Earth's." (from; Origins, Tyson and Goldsmith/ Norton, NY. 2004)

Suggestion may forward the idea of a maturing or evolving cosmos with no time / linear interpretation other than the temporarily useful one here exhibited in rationality.

"De-coupling, is a term describing action of a universe changing from an homogenous subatomic energy sea, (Dark chaos) into a clumpy, point-energy initiated cosmos, illustrating forms of complexity," perhaps with boundaries set out by influence of gravity wave. (Wikipedia) Further elaboration will be discussed in design of "perpetuity principle."

Encarta Dictionary states that "fodder" is an expendable ingredient that makes a system work. An Earthly example may be of earth itself. It is same molecules of dirt being used over and over in donation to various new or distinct creations and life forms.

Rationalism may be a cosmic example of fodder in a greater scheme.

"If field aura of necessarily expendable ingredient of planned purpose is accentuated as an "aesthetic" quality then contribution in such a worship will mature that for which purpose exists." (Encarta) To be discussed again in greater detail.

The participatory idea forwards a "direction" that may illustrate Greg Braden's "Quantum Dialogue" a conversation of "unfinished business."

> Braden: "Depest belief becomes a phenomenal blueprint and forwards what will mature into choice of experience."

> Corbin: "Imaginational beings and events are part of projecting experience and have been so since organic rationalism."

Hesiod first used the term "chaos" about 3,000 yrs. ago to describe a principle, referring to the source of creation. Dark chaos energy has a sort of benign neutrality containing all possible projection, be that subjectively considered positive or negative. Access is via a common key and becomes the "journey," with intent, heart's desire, motive and will, planted as seeds of occupation. In maturation and achievement, contribution and eventuality will establish energetic donation.

Similar to a Pythagorean lecture, the Carpadia series will ever so gradually unveil a beyond cosmic overview and ascertain a balance of rational organic with it. Though miniscule, contribution of rationality is "aesthetic" and as such is cumulatively fundamental.

> So,...A Place with no Name, (inside nuclear furnace) may be described, but not "known."
> ....The farthest reaches of a visible cosmos may be seen or heard but never touched.
> ....A nuclear furnace may come into being in order to create rational organic.

….Worship as achievement aesthetically embellishes Dark chaos energy.

….A cosmic striving with untold disciplines surplus Dark to develop critical state.

….An irritant is introduced to a homeostatic saturation. As a perturbation a gravity wave rent tears vacuum energy at pressure membrane. Obtrusive frequencies are strained at point creation and in case, of rational organic the all familiar photon pulse is revealed.

….The un-namable comes into temporality and beauty as aesthetic is described.

"Novelty" brings investment from critical reservoir via imposition into action. Un-measurable, therefore instantaneous process of a billion eons advances gravity wave rent induced photon pulse from status of point energy to that of nuclear furnace. Much later, compilation of star dust and molecule that is rational organic emerges. Eventual circulation of worship as "dirt" of rational fodder achieves aesthetic contribution. Re-saturation of a re-building homogenous system "precinct" again contributes toward critical state.

Miniscule percentile that rational organic holds dear is almost insignificant other than worship accumulative. Remembering that contribution of "familiar persuasion" is only one of the ones.

One might envision an instantaneously timeless circle of perpetually plural one. If there is no concept of measurement then it does not exist. Without the "rational" aspect, time, distance and position evaluation are meaningless impossibilities.

How could a billion eons be contained in an instant? Each moment of aesthetic worship achieves and contributes. A billion eons of homeostatic benign neutrality do not. Perhaps the other side of an immeasurable, full of other "non-familiar" clumps of star dust begin to demonstrate their own forms of complexity, beauty and worship.

Gravity rent is a tear in wholeness and oneness of Dark chaos at a kind of pressure membrane. It manifests as point creation and eventually blesses the rational "one" with a fractal of chaos possibility. Later discussed in detail,….. this is key.

Gravity rent - forward photon to nuclear furnace - eventual rational being - aesthetic embellishment - critical chaos precinct - gravity rent.

Turner's God in "Faith Seeking": "God is profoundly apophatic wholly other and in the end unknowable darkness." Deep, eternally proximal Dark chaos energy sea of possibility has no location, size, visibility or parameter.

These are of the "untouchables." They are similar to farthest corners of cosmos or quirky, otherworldly realm just next to absolute zero.

Are there squiggles evident in gravity lensing? Is that cosmic background radiation singing in the cochlea? Is there an acrid testimonial of assimilated morose product re-issuing disgust in animal organics?

Contact/interaction is most prevalent and binding and in fact quantum theory says it is the "only" process occurring. Homogeny of chaos can only be relevant to totality of chaos with the exception of a fractal key. Dark chaos energy is constantly receiving a barrage of contribution from billions of "ones." They may be watching, listening and feeling,…therefore participating.

Very small and unique "parcels" or "precincts" of Chaos, (perhaps those with donations from "familiar" rational organics) may be relatively empty, or bursting with potential. Critical saturation may not need to occur across the board and hence many proximal critical saturations may occur.

"If life begins and dies out repeatedly while chaos rains down through creation point processes by which "life" may originate seem robust. One might expect them to have/will occur again and again, perhaps in other "situation" work moments." (adapted from "Origins", Tyson and Goldsmith)

As gravity rent is introduced it "attracts" from similar precincts and that action must be contained according to "familiars." Armature, or path has been relevant within framework of instigation. Scaffold is in place as sculpture begins. Just as in any earthly example, from totem poles to Greek gods, the aesthetically pleasing and meaningful with suggestion and purpose of worship is within Dark chaos, red cedar or granite block.

Creation of life experience is an artistic process of revealing, by focus, attention and limitation. Work moment is "realized" energy transfer there-by attributing aesthetic. In rational organics this "quality" can only return to source, relinquishing identity and has no other function. Without rationality, time does not exist. With it there is an instant of being and worship. It has that moment of contribution forever, by being in attendance (identity) once. It has "happened" and cannot again be found.

There may be a systematic "participation" of novelty constantly within chaos,…. "standing by,"…… in order to forward perpetuity.

It is not magical but is "Magik" de-constructing God mountain hidden in fog, to rational fog unveiled and presenting an ultimately simplistic God-mountain moment. Creation as a process of artistic limitation should not suggest settling points. It may necessitate a reading through all phenomenal dynamic possibility to that great divine unity within a corner of every moment.

> A systematic
> Participation
> Of Novelty
> Within Chaos
> To forward perpetuity.

Network……… widely distributed inter-relation of signal and response

Scheme……….. an intent to forward "action"(necessary fodder)

Achievement….. earning manifest potential of probable dynamic

Orientation……. position proposal,…reactive direction of stimulus. Methodical, organized, habitual macro-taxonomy?

When in query with perpetuity one must only consider participatory "in function." Involving Dark energy sea of possibility as maximum potential suggests maximum "in function." Though it is not,….. realizing exponential to the utmost propagation of triggers, … magnitude of fractal cosmic extrapolation is undone by complexity, though key remains.

The only requirement may be to advance through veils and beyond settling points. They are primary building blocks of hive and are well maintained. All disciplines of worker bees contribute to quality and longevity of hive. Hive is not,….. way of the Fifth.

There is a realm of contributory fragments that surface here and there and must continue to do so. These may be in names of the "Homeric Path" and may be seekers of Heart's desire. This situation is leaning toward maximum contributory aesthetic of being.

Suppose a situation when a potentiality wave begins to break over rationality without finding harbor, commerce or trade. Suppose light house signal dims. In such a circumstance total "hive" idea may have to rest in chaos. Yet,…all ideas rest in chaos. Wave of possibility is also within hive, not clearly visible as hive behavior, but carried by every "one" of the participants.

A free "ticket" is to be aware of how that is accomplished and the extreme price that can and has so often been paid by not knowing. (locally described as,….. selling the soul)

What a Holy, Aboriginal, ancient Egyptian, Chinese, Hindu, Persian, Zoroastrian, Rosicrucian, and perhaps Disney scoop.

There is an idea of perpetuity that is evident everywhere and every-when but not so blatant under the glaring energy spectrum of "now." Furthest cosmic reaches are relative to temporality and must be equated with present. Even point created origin of this and all other universes are apparently time relative.

Perpetuity is "on the other side" of a pressure energy membrane. In it a question such as,….how many one's? …..is invalid, as that would require a finitude.

Perpetuity must be an ever broadening "phrasing" of aesthetic.

Allowing worship of "being" as a contributory quality is "sharing" regardless of magnitude of discrepancy in ratio of expression/non-expression. This is macro creating micro whose miniscule individual contribution helps to allow macro to create.

Rational organic is realm of contributory fragment and great Dark chaos storm, is nest of perpetuity principle.

There must be an elite "bridge" unseen and equally vague in location, size and parameter. One might name this access key.........."soul."

It may be a fractal extrapolation of Dark chaos energy and as such would be able to harbor with rationality and may with precious attention be able to extend to unlimited contributors of whatever design. Method of donation would also be integral. When experience is complete a "common" vitality without identity remains in reservoir of possibility.

Any situation, "familiar" or not might be valid confirmation of the sharing,…. and Big Bang or God may only be puffs of wind in a perpetual chaos maelstrom of pulsating pressure variant homogeny as cauldron of eternity.

Perhaps there is only, as Holy Trinity,… gravity wave trigger,… effecting pressure reservoir…. to create point. That may be a fundamental of perpetuity principle.

"Pressure"…a force that "urges persuasively" in critical potentiality or possibility.

Gravity-wave that induces rent as an irritant.

Sand in a sand realm is a place-holder, not an essential for pearl development. Sand in an organic realm is irritant that is wrapped in layers of pearl.

Awareness in an awareness realm is a place-holder, not an essential for time development. Awareness in an organic realm is irritant that is wrapped in layers of time.

Gravity wave in a gravity wave realm is a place-holder, not an essential for creation. Gravity wave in a pressurized chaos potentiality is an irritant that describes point, and is wrapped in layers of creation.

Gravity wave does not follow as a ripple in space-time, but develops a space-time ripple. "The presence of a gravity wave brings the concept of a "limiting" speed of propagation of physical or phenomenal interaction with it." Wikipedia (Lorentz invariance of General Relativity)

A limiting velocity of familiar, neighborhood phenomena would be speed of light. It may only be one of the ones. Within process of rational organic it is quite sustainable and functional, perhaps as evolutionary necessity of direction toward rational organic. It has afforded an opportunity to marry, have offspring, buy a house, retire and leave the kids something in your will,..... and to hunt, search, delve and rummage in conceptual perpetuity principle. Second choice is not as popular as first.

An energy meniscus is maintained by surface tension, very similar to the tensile pressure at a voltage gated ion channel. One side, fecund chaos sea and the other, a method of enhancing that with aesthetic. Proximal realms of allegoric absurdity of atmosphere and ocean.

Superior suggestion and purpose principle may be "tracked" by prayer. Intention of tracking is unveiling and ludicrous subtlety is a "sharing" at interface.

Within possibility reservoir there may be discrepancies of density, pressure and contribution, as worship without identity. A wave irritant at membrane interface would be a "surface" gravity wave rent developing point, while a wave orbit between gravity precincts, "internal" and not developing point. Breaking wave collapsing into point is beach-head of creation. Simultaneously initiating a capacity for development at an incredible exponential expansion rate it is introduction of "point momentum" and will not brake until nuclear furnace and complexity, worship and contribution have been achieved.

It is a bold prayer that can never be localized. Magikal disguise may intuit a dhow nudging across the membrane, just barely leaving wake. An extended palm of query may allow tasting the chaos salt-lick and hiding within a particle/wave interval. It may bring a unique confidence in non-locality, the true field camouflage of the hunter.

The message was beyond equilibrium and never intended to be seen. It was not for flock or school but was for those who would be confidently ushered into that which they inherently feared,...not for moms and dads but for those who would seek the high road.

"An experiential whisper is experimental mayhem in subtle world fragment of point evolution awareness and Dark chaos extrapolation, from gravity wave rent of critical precinct pressure in reservoir." It may or may not succeed. Many creation points do not.

Where is the fodder?
How are irritants introduced?
Why only pressure, trigger and point?
What about prayer?
When is time possible?

Intent of trail, print or wake is in reading. If it was worldly one would follow it to that which had left it. If it is not phenomenal one must track in the opposite direction to source of that which had left it.

It is not looking for presence of "situation" but for its intent. "Situation" could/would only appear with purpose.

Similar to outback aboriginals, a verse or song is required. Perhaps a "yarn" played out as one investigates the labyrinth. At Kiijay's first tracking of the wolf's intent verse was necessary in an unchanging landscape that did not absorb any spectral frequencies, just as time is necessary in an unchanging landscape of infinite frequencies.

Both, and in fact all such pilgrimage is "un-veiling," and that is of necessity "sharing." Perhaps via a Magik shaman gate into perpetuity concept with non-locality, a description of sharing may result. It is merely re-iterating verse-song furnace trail that evolution has left with a not so subtle wake,…with intent.

A "parallax" is apparent change of position of situation when a description of situation changes. (Encarta) Of course, any distancing is perspective,…point to point, prayer to prayer, situation to situation or creation to creation. In distancing of point, prayer or situation may be a spiritual parallax. Complexity of rational organic in experience, involves achievement worship and contribution. Describing situation involves change. Change is of a river flowing past a fixed point. Point does not change but the perception of it is of continuous variability due to flow.

"Situation" only appears with purpose and in a perpetuity loop, that may simply be contribution as aesthetic.

Fodder is at energy membrane of a bulbous pressure confined Dark sea of chaos vitality.

9

Irritants are introduced by uniquely imaginative characteristic of gravity wave.

Simplicity endures.

Prayer, …is involving oneself with perpetuity. To seek and delve into "source." Prayer is rational organic "method" in recognizing perspective within flow.

When is time possible?…..Perfect!

In reflection: "Time is necessary in the unchanging landscape of infinite frequencies." It may be verse, song and yarn, and must be method prayer of "sharing."

When is one not one?….never….one is always one and unlimited plural one is one. "Sharing" is binary and is place holder column and one. It will flourish into contribution, achievement and worship and in a spectacular, unique aesthetic quality will beautify perpetuity. (because it has "happened") By supplying energy that in "familiar" donor precinct will non-directionally inflate, as in buoyancy,….. gravity will eventually try to compensate via wave rent.

Homogeny and equilibrium are not mundane in perpetuity. (as Quantum theory has described) In familiar cosmic theater the simple principle will always endure, and extrapolation may occur in either direction of entropy arrow.

Perpetual system of a grandest scale will always have untold resource of energy reservoir that is unavailable to do work. (for example any that does not involve "moment") and that which may be between precincts and not effected by gravity wave rent at critical energy membrane.

This is energy that keeps the perpetual pump "primed."

As with cosmic, so with organic.

After "realization" a mother gives all of her available resource over to a new creation. A fodder principle inhibited the created and incubation concept from infiltrating too deeply into survival source and "limited" point creation.

Gravity, nuclear and evolutionary noise efficiency irritants may balance to utilize creative spring and always leave energy pump "primed."

This balance could also be maintained by idea that time will end. There can be no sustained time in perpetuity but its occurrence as "situation" allows "sharing" and contribution "when it is possible."

Continuous time is continuous contribution and that would not "work."

Continuous process of gravity rent is continuous pressure vent and that would not "work."

Continuous Holy Trinity is the active (pressure, trigger, point) perpetuity principle that "works."

From isospin to isostasy. (not far in a dictionary)

"Value" in point developed electro-magnetic micro-environment and in blueprint of fractal edge of a snowflake contributing to Arctic ice shelf, is acknowledgement in "presence" be it extraordinary pressure or infinitesimal charge. Is it valuable information?.. perhaps only in "work moment," but is not all information the scat of that which has left it? (intending reading) Prayer, as track (sharing) has always relied on that, in physics or philosophy, religion or spirituality.

But what in value of a philosophy of "qualitative state" be it in micro/isospin or macro/isostasy. Hebrew Microprosopos and Macroprosopos,...A small visage with enduring universal rhythm and the larger with hidden "qualitative" side. Smaller named God and larger named "I am." (from "Hero with a Thousand Faces")

What in "value" of, as Robert Brandon has stated, "creation and conveyance of conceptual understanding of features involving only conceptual understanding." These are not micro or macro, spacial, temporal, spectral, stellar or cosmic. Are they imaginary? Where is value? That is the point. It is contribution via rationality of an aesthetic quality and is both recognition of beauty and beast, love and war.

War pulls one out of order and into a fierce chaos. Experience of it is huge contribution directly into chaos reservoir.

It is contribution of "value" in any familiar particle-wave medium, as one of the ones, that inflates a precinct energy node in extremely vast homogeny of a perpetuity loop, not able to affect such a contribution by life or consciousness without.

Value is in prayer,…involving oneself with perpetuity. It is "rational" organic method in recognizing distance from situation to situation and if desired is upon Homeric Path, even with only philosophical conceptual understanding. Not abstract, but in realm of civilization, and objective is to move all of that toward the Fifth.

If one's heart's desire is realization of alternative situation, then one must move into alternative situation.

"Let us call that beautiful of which the apprehension in itself,… pleases." (St. Thomas Aquainus)

It is aesthetic and is beauty, is war and is assimilation. It is so extremely basal that it may be, "eat and be eaten." It is charge, volume, mass and imagination, dream and myth. As method prayer of "sharing" it is verse-song-yarn unveiling value of action in presence of rationality. No contribution of beauty can be made without realizing eye of beholder.

If an organic system of synaptic chaos can be tamed by frequency spectrum then a type of yoke will affect and direct "work moment." When the system of synaptic chaos is tamed by "conceptual" therapy, there may be an opportunity of transcending yoke. It may be in periphery of value of prayer. Looking at it is a blind spot, but assimilating the wiggles and squiggles around it becomes a very personal journey to the Fifth. Wiggles and squiggles may have naively been named "string theory" in physics but it/they are never the less fodder for opportunity to display. "It" will not differentiate from oneness or wholeness. Necessary and expendable ingredient that makes Holy Trinity as scheme of perpetuity, is not only conceptual, but can even be heard in the sound of silver threads in cosmic background radiation. Is there limit,…. resting point,…. End?

There will always be re-animation of nuclear furnace by gravity rent in a Dark incomprehensible when pressure is targeted by trigger to display point. (all energy may come from point)

The gravity of Magik builds in "a place with no name." Its activating principle (pressure) is warmed with energy contribution of billions of ones. Increase…not decision, only choice,…and spark/rent creates a situation. It immediately has purpose. It is intrinsically perfect and causal and will produce result. It is point-basis of "action" toward reason and flourishing of worship and contribution. (perhaps)

Gravity always wins contrivance of realm creation. Is it nuclear furnace that causes extreme temperature and pressure or the extreme temperature from exhausting pressure that causes nuclear furnace?

In point-energy-creation scheme "lighter" less dense, perhaps fundamental or Godly elements are consumed or assimilated and the bit of particle residue and ash with increasing influences of "heavier" and more complex, may begin to form that which in several billion years of temporality will contribute. (as in fodder or star dust)

Bruno Giordano, the greatest self-proclaimed heretic of the Inquisition had a movingly simply statement about creation. "All thing are made of God, not just by God." Pythagoras of Samos,...."all souls are kin."

Any one of ones will manifest from Dark chaos pressure accumulation of contributing ones inflating precinct pressure aesthetically until critical state introduces gravity rent to open point.

There is harmony within cosmic soul and with fractal extrapolation of all souls. "One" might strive for personal harmony in realization of divine percentage. Away from bright lights and calamity and within contemplative moment a citizen of the Fifth may move closer to Dark commission. This would be creative energy paid oneself over rate of initial investment. After achievement and contribution,..... this is confidence, wisdom and grace.

(true aesthetic qualities)

Any recognizable frequency spectrum created and influenced by gravity is neither infinite, Godly nor perpetual. Dark chaos reservoir is fodder. Time is verse-song of silver threads and conceptual pressure/gravity/point relation is perpetuity principle.

Heracitus of Ephesus.... "one cannot step twice into the same river for new waters are ever flowing." It is such with perpetuity. All contribution is without identity and aesthetics suggest just that.

Beauty is thus realized with beholder, not by donor.

Achievement is subjectively unrecognizable but by temporality as a process of "reflecting" upon self. (identity of form appears in mirror although it is not in mirror) When, as is necessary for perpetuity principle, that "situation" is concluded donation ceases but beauty of it is beheld. This is contributory because in time-line-verse it has "happened" and out of time-line-verse any "happening" must be considered an embellishment or flourishing.

Resistance against the river is "identifying" but any other step or re-entry does not carry that with. The river is different at any identity point. "One" identity can never step twice, nor a million times. It happens with one occasion. "What is an apparent change of situation when description of situation changes?"…..(a parallax) Perhaps it is time to re-focus, not upon step but upon river.

Democritis,…philosopher of "atoma" and void. (460BC-370BC)

"Atoms are invisible to the naked eye and indivisible. All phenomena contain atoma and a measure of Dark void within. An apple is easier to cut then a stone because it contains a larger portion of void.

Senses and ability to reason, in rational organic preserve a limit of existence amid atoma and energy flow of river from exhausting pressure of chaos possibility. That resistance is "being" and results in identity. Fundamental principle immediately results in purpose. Philosophic and conceptual ideas are still of reasonable or rational nature and contribute as does love and hate. They are aesthetic, though un-manifest."

Vortex of necessity in perpetuity.

A vortex in proximity of water carries water and a vortex in proximity of sand carries sand, so does a vortex in proximity of necessity carry necessity? It is involution of focal "point" that if possibly imaginable could include every one of the ones in a unilateral vortex.

This is probably not of demand but of service.
It will be innate in perpetuity.

Flourishing in rational macrocosm.
Flourishing in irrational macrocosm.
Microprosopos and Macroprosopos.
The smaller named God and the larger…I am.
Break the spell.

Simple,.....push Dark.

Flourishment as a herald of enthusiasm, announcement of presence by rational organic and trusting prayer as a yarn, rhyme or time story will suggest the Fifth.

An idea of an energy origami is unveiled. One encompassing dimension of chaos, acted upon by trigger to form complexity and diversity. The very necessary settling of point is that time of each enfolding and unfolding in each incredible aesthetic will end. It must in order to keep perpetuity loop in recurrence.

Not of request or demand, but of service
Ceremony of worship and prayer
Ritual involving self with divinity
Performed in extreme variety, yet possibly prescribed form
A step into the river

The awesome reality is that rational organic need not orchestrate, or even comprehend in order for the scheme to work and flourish through diverse time references. Verse-song is method prayer of "sharing' between rational organic and divine principle. This personal, intimate dialogue is a "service." It is "work moment" the experience of "being" done in reciprocity with aesthetic contribution toward an idea of divine unity and purpose.

D.C. Bennett adapted from, "Breaking the Spell,".....'It might be that God implants each rational being with an immortal soul (Dark moment) that thirsts for opportunity to worship God. (Dark eternity) Did God set up a universe so that rational organic would evolve to love and worship God?"

Design of perpetuity has no author, creator, inventor, editor or even critic. It has always and will always be. Situation is proof. It is pressure via aesthetic contribution, trigger of gravity wave rent as irritant and point,..... the necessity of creation.

"Differential replication" is Ibn¢ Arabi's "recurrence of the like but not same." Some of energy contribution from "familiar" energy node precinct without identity, will help create similar point situation, perhaps capable of evolving into achievement and a flourishing,…. or perhaps not. Of billions of nuclear furnaces in various stages of growth or decay, very few will, though there is still a very positive contributory factor.

So creation as a "one" and place holder displays well when it does "happen' across an infinite background. A competent accountant may record the ledger with or without judgement, passion or joy, yet simply in the act of recording is appropriate energy contribution as aesthetic.

D.C. Bennett inquires after a rational God center and reciprocity for that revealed investment. He asks; …What is purpose and value? Why did it evolve with rational organic?

Purpose is supported by value of contribution. It has been manipulated by religious God center activists, but proceeding in matters of importance, has already "happened." Perhaps God center has evolved with "corner in Dark moment" that sings praise of Dark chaos fodder of possibility. Soul singing praise of Divinity.

In a simplicity of ideas that might seem to work, a God center in situation of rational organic may only be that Dark corner in an almost completely saturated "print" of temporality, and its complex though finite multitudes of frequency.

Rational organic, aware of beauty and war, love and hate, good and evil is,… in aesthetic of "happening" contributing with or along with that finite,…toward the infinite. Millions of universes that simply burn out do not contribute, but by fodder.

A multitude of ones achieving awareness of contribution increase pressure at nodes of similar energy supplement. Trigger of gravity rent (irritant) begged for by critical buoyancy occurs at this amplitude, this largeness, this distance from "mean" or at this maximum "value." There is a creating intersection and re-creating point and messenger, first sending into "being" and then receiving love, hate and worship from it as aesthetic.

This principle of perpetuity is expensive.

Adapted from: "Price inversion Effect" Starke and Finke (2000)

"Cost of interaction is one factor in any exchange, quality of product and service are others and together they yield an estimate of "value." Strength of a higher degree of distinctiveness, separation and psychic cost is that it offers greater value and is able to do so because it is more expensive.

Cult of the rational organic is high in material, social intellectual and emotional cost, much higher than animal or plant world. "Belonging" requires constant payment and yet value is evident in extraordinary aspect of recognizable experience." (rationality)

Coming into comprehension of perpetuity principle and its expense and value will maximise a level of confidence in absolute fundamental cosmos.

It costs more then heaven but gives greater value and still provides for eternal bliss. (minus identity)

Benefit received in rationality is awareness of experience contribution and the otherworld promise of religion has already been validated by physics.....energy cannot be created or destroyed. Energy of "being" will continue. In need of more experiential reward? Live freely within light. It is more available than ever, yet often obscured by a low cost and hence low value, boring neighborhood situation.

One might suggest a low value situation replacing the already cheap circumstance of professional dogma.

Adapted from: ... Bowles and Gintis (98/01)

"Pro-social but weaker confidence strengths are effect dependent on low cost access to information about other community members as well as tendency to favor interactions with group members and restrict migration in and out." Social media has become much more important than any religious suggestion or formal faith or educational institution. The low cost, low value situation invites low confidence and low self esteem. When responsibility is diffused across access more expensive principles, suggestions and ideas may simply not be entertained.

Even if confronted with such an awareness,.... that secret would have to be kept until it went away.

The idea of expulsion from social media is intolerable,.... Similar to the idea of expulsion from church in previous generations. So an idea of "presence" or "acceptance" in low cost social media or religion is equated with a strict circle of peers. (that only allow entry via recommendation)

Strength of higher distinctiveness, separation and psychic energy carries far greater value and is again able to do so because it is more expensive.

Any individual ritual involving one-self as a "presence" with divinity must be a very personal, high cost situation and must describe greater value.

Product or service is this intimate dialogue. It is not a humble step but a single leap of faith into the cosmic river that defines a beautiful contributory identity of achievement.

Schooling of fish, flocking of birds or religious or social network systems allow a security for an individual within, …..yet outside of group, vulnerability of any "one" is extreme.

Sanctity of any and all of these groups is that at a very basic level of survival, procreation and maturity,… a process of "belonging" is endorsed by cosmic evolution from point creation to rational organic.

At the end result of rationality and awareness of experience there may be the ability to leave the flock in confidence without pre-mature devolution into chaos. It carries a subtle strength of invulnerable freedom within the light.

It is not, nor should be protected by an armor coat but is never the less untouchable within that extreme self-confidence of being alone, knowing that aloneness in cosmos and loving that very unique dialogue of aesthetic contribution.

Once it has "happened" occurrence will be embraced by cosmic essence. Time will come and go with similar occurrences and any situation will embellish. The achievement, as earlier suggested, is without identity and accumulates as a kind of pressure. Critical precinct buoyancy begs for gravity rent to create point and advance the maturing scheme. This is perpetuity principle.

Why is rational organic and ability to reason a perceived end point?…. it is not,….but it may be a turning point. As a solar system may traverse the lateral cusp of a galaxy, so may an accountability of rationality tumble over that edge. Perhaps some ideas are getting more expensive. What does Greg say?.....Push.

> Is it true that causality can never be found within a system?
> Is it potency within capacity which may cause accordingly?
> Does a concept of balance position potential into probability?
> How does perpetuity principle reckon with regard?

What is a sequence of binary encounters that can have effect on continuous replication? Cosmic Dark chaos substrates, as one of the ones may be extremely varied. Abstract symbolic projection may be an only exemplar and may prove rather "stable" between "times." "Seed" of a replicator may be independent, movable and storable.

If there is intent in causality this "seed" may be a deliberate, kind of seasonal instigator. Perpetuity principle may allow propagules grace of a freedom in development, depending on pressure.

Potency within capacity may gain access to replication process when/where critical pressure landscapes are in proximity.

Ability to question is expensive. Daniel Bennett adapted from "Breaking the Spell," ....There is a hypothesis that curiosity is costly and when it cannot pay for itself by guiding, tracking or sourcing, then it is abandoned. Did rationality begin with a question or an answer,... or was it the answer to its own question?

A question is a request, as in prayer of God seeking prayer of man,... as in Dark pressure of chaos seeking gravity rent to create point.

An answer is an active response, prayer of man, irritant of rent upon fodder of possibility to begin creation and quest of rationality.

Adapted preface by Harold Bloom of "Alone with the Alone." (Princeton press 1997): "Prayer is a means of existing and causing to exist. Dark God asking for understanding in recognizable frequency spectrum of work moment. It is an epiphany of "it" by presence. Energy of existentiation of all universal being that is knowable.

Prayer of man evolved from point eventually brings active and creative imagination and query of rationality into being, and measure of that capacity is achievement. Form suggests beginning and end but all are perpetually engendered."

The principle is totality. It cannot be directly spoken of from presence. Some historical religious dogmas have prohibited speaking the name of God.

Aesthetics in form happen in ever more complex situation. "All are systematic, canonic, essential characteristic patterns of solar, point based, phenomena. It unveils all aesthetic creation and may even push into abstract proofs of mathematics, science, hypothesis, philosophy and perhaps even emotion." (The Rattlesnake School : Jose¢ Diaz Bollo)

These categories exist although they do not contribute by physical aesthetic. Do emotions "happen" and philosophy, heroes and mythology,...what about theoretical mathematics? Bringing order with reason is a consequence of rationality.

Light as a limited form contained within Dark.

Order as work moment form, contained within chaos.

So if purpose of rationality is contribution then "order" is means of achievement and successful aesthetic contributor.

As many in various disciplines would offer,...if there becomes an understanding of basis of perpetuity principle, one would have to embrace a suggestion of freedom within light. That may be a base-line intention of effort and may be valid preparation for the Fifth.

As in "The Evolution of God"; (Robert Wright) and "Breaking the Spell"; (D.C. Bennett)......the three significant Abrahamic religions have been investigated sufficiently to realize that the mythological and historic influences have been negated, simplified or ignored in order to maintain faith and belief in supernatural beings that interact with the rational organic. These are stories carefully edited and re-written to maintain a supreme being. (no personal responsibility)

As in science of atom, photon, quark and quantum. At the most intense levels of investigation there is becoming a realization that the nature of rational description is a limited process. It will not apply to extremely micro/macro, cold/hot, then/now, or here/there. The community of such sleuths are banging particles into each other in proton cathedrals to find evidence of a supreme being. (God particle)

The Fifth should not entertain either in any form of ones.

It will be a civilization accepting responsibility for comprehension of human condition. When global, simple and in balance it will be "touched" by a greater then universal awareness.

An alien civilization accepting responsibility for the comprehension of its condition, when global, simple and in balance will also be "touched" by the same greater then universal awareness.

The electro-magnetic spectrum is "one" of methodic, systematic principles within Dark chaos vacuum energy. This is "stuff" of rational destiny. Myriad complexities of contribution are universally displayed and although not generally accepted due to subjective criteria, apparent negative and positive contribute occur equally and alike.

In purest form of action as aesthetic there is definitely no such idea in the cosmos as "good" and "evil."

When civilization became aware of cosmic order, or that order influenced movement into civilization, heavenly bodies became rational and God was born. Rationality moves in an orderly way and differentiation contributes. All or any of chaos will not move until a God is introduced. That results in creation and that furthers achievement and that in occurring contributes aesthetically and that inflates precinct chaos possibility until gravity rent opens point. That is perpetuity principle.

That point can be the source of all power in a universe. A resulting billion year plan may be to evolve into an order or differentiation of contribution. Process has no measurement of years until rationality brings temporality.

What actually "occurs" is value in moment and moments are only assigned station in/by aesthetics.

An aesthetic station of value, from thermo-nuclear point to rational organic must be recognized in occurrence of consecutive moments and rationality provides just that in retrospect.

But perhaps soul holds or is held by a corner of Dark realm that is not rational cosmos, not order and not aesthetic and when those criteria are removed, Dark immovable chaos remains,...... slightly embellished.

(by the happening) Higher purpose is imparted by something quite different from a God,...... as Gods are traditionally conceived.

If a scheme displays as a system, primary recognition is still point and maturing universe evolution toward rational organic as aesthetic occurrence may replicate more efficiently then universe evolution toward situation that lacks this sort of order. In perpetuity that may result in a maturing type of evolution toward rational aesthetic occurrence contributing to non-identity pressure that is precinct orientated by or in response to a "successful" formula of replication.

In a quantum or cosmological wording or a theological extrapolation one might take a leap of faith, or electron leap, to ask to what extent "growth" might occur and how might that be important?

It has been suggested in many disciplines that growth may be evidence of purpose. It is not equilibrium and must leave track in equilibrium. Because evidence may be regarded as a statement of witness, "it" the parameter of growth must be of an aesthetic quality of recognizable happening enhancing a divine, incorporeal and immaterial criteria with a capacity for all creation. With such purpose there is always an "argument" that may not allow permission for spatial expression.

One might have to employ all manner of myth, allegory and reason, from theology, legend and science in order to suggest, hint or imply such a non-existence.

Growth, as...leaving track in equilibrium,...has intent of being read and that "planned purpose" is made evident in "order" to provide "reason" for/to rational organic.

This recognition offers a subtle empowering tranquil silence within every moment. The culture of physics clearly suggests and defends an ever-present "interval of light." (Dark corner?) Living freely within electro-magnetic spectrum may mean holding a miniscule understanding of an inexpressible that is not attached, blocked or restricted by spectrum. Perhaps a soul may be, or be in the embrace of a portion of Dark energy that each rational organic "possesses" within interval of spectrum that is not cosmos, order or aesthetic.

It may be unique incidence of "ownership" that separates one's progression of apparent consecutive moment from all others. Properties of light are shared, but properties of Dark wholeness are not, …while in cosmic order. That might be the plural ones differentiation of wholeness. When that criteria is no longer, all is again a slightly embellished, by aesthetic separatism of happening,…..as one.

Recognize permission to embrace such a creation foundation without science or theology and fulfilment may be a necessary consequence.

Philo was a great thinker of ancient times. His world view was in blending the theological literature of the YAHWEH school with the philosophical/scientific approach of Athenian Greece. He equated the term "logos" with "wisdom" of biblical "proverbs" or "sirach."

Author Robert Wright "The Evolution of God" asks if the kind of "wisdom" common rational organics possess, is wholly different from a "wisdom" that God possesses. In answering, he says that the Philonic world view suggests a continuity.

* How could, God/perpetuity principle, have set up logos/order of being so that "wisdom" found in the evidence/witness of macro and hidden in moment corner of micro may, with careful report and diligence (track in equilibrium, therefore growth) be revealed as unity.

"Sharing" that truth with Divinity may be an empowering enlightenment of subtly beauty,…an aesthetic quality illustrating huge achievement and hence unprecedented contribution to same Divine principle. The "knowing" as greatest compliment of foundation scheme of creation will be,….fulfilment.

A scheme accords or renders moment participation in/where rational pursuit may seek wisdom/Dark proximally, as self-seeking interest and at the beyond of cosmic Divinity.

At chaos soul with order and at perpetuity principle.

Philo writes that design is of a "straight high road," that with one adept at reading track (that which has been left by growth) and perhaps a little guidance, wisdom, logos, method or scheme may be known in the "sharing." Only in that process may a pilgrim navigate such a lofty pursuit with intent,… and hence discover that which has purposely left track. (in "order" to be discovered) For ancients it was personified or deified with the logos as Lady Wisdom or Sophia. For a seeker of the

Fifth it may also be abstract, as in pushed further then commonality (no settling) toward,…

"an inseparable portion of Divine and Blessed Soul." (Philo)

In a cosmos and soul that cannot truthfully differentiate negative or positive contribution, …in purest form of "action" as aesthetic,… there is no such idea as good or evil. War and love are subjective situations of equal and alike, as they simply will have occurred. That will leave track on equilibrium, and embellish Dark chaos possibility with intent of being read as planned purpose,…… suggesting reason and recognizing growth.

That is accepted until perhaps a critical precinct abundance of familiar contribution, when an efficient replicating process again introduces gravity rent and as such insertion of point.

Perhaps "growth" of perpetuity principle (God) will confirm existence of perpetuity principle. (God)

Aesthetic contribution of "being" begins when a rational organic arrives and ends when a rational organic departs. In that achievement as evidence of higher purpose use of the term divinity may be supported.

Theologies of the world were personified and deified and scientific communities strived for different abstract labels. So be it.

A seeker of the Fifth must realize that they are only one of the ones, an end line of evolution, created to worship, contribute and maintain a perpetual principle of divinity and to push an understanding beyond the God of religion.

Is soul simply a miniscule portion of Dark chaos, (as fractal extrapolation) that is interval of light present in every moment?

Is "reasoning" simply ability to continually skip over obvious hiccups in "order" to advance continuity of achievement and embellish by aesthetics of occurrence. All "happenings" are of like but not same, but Dark soul energy is always the same, within or without.

Adapted from Robert Wright,…. "The Evolution of God," ….. "human beings are organic machines that are built by natural selection to deal with other organic machines. Understanding, visualizing and loving with worship of divinity may be a tall order for a mere human being."

Yet a seeker of the Fifth knows that soul is of a divine nature. (Dark energy) If such a pilgrim can ignore settling points of science and theology and aspire toward "the high straight road," a "sharing" may become evidence of contribution to higher principle.

If such a scheme is made evident in rationality it will have probably been saturated with purpose.

Evolving point to rational organic is a procedure, the algorithm of which may be well established in instantaneous billions of uncountable years. This entire scheme of "being" may be only one "design" with purpose of aesthetic occurrence and hence embellishment.

It is a replicating, "exquisitely directional" process and because it may occur with predictability, repetitive success may be a common "contribution corridor" of energy in perpetuity.

Such a system of being rational organic may mature in quantity and quality. Sheer numbers and aesthetic achievement, of a global complex, functioning integrated system, affording much more enhanced energy manipulation and therefore more efficient pay-back of aforementioned energy loan of "becoming,"…. first initiated at gravity rent investment, creating point,…. will embellish exponentially.

A miniscule "labor of love" was begun and then differentiated, evolved and naturally selected to painstakingly mature into rational organic, capable of worship and contribution.

To,….."recognize" (Encarta World Dictionary) …identify and acknowledge achievement, to reward, to accept validity and truth.

A rational organic of the Fifth recognizes creative energy of being rational organic and loan begins vitality re-payment with interest, contributing to growth of chaos reservoir. (not equilibrium therefore with purpose)

Albert Einstein:….."curiosity has its own reason for existing."

Maturing, questioning, developing energy of modern rational organic may have greatly favored investment opportunity due to a type of equity in the value of a repetitively successful scheme,….as a "property" of sorts.

The industry of loaning energy, by perpetuity principle (God) has a familiar analogue in a current monetary (banking) system.

Hermes:…….. "as above, so below."

One might look for other Godly properties in the familiar.

If a creation scheme is saturated with purpose and rational organic has its own creation scheme to observe, it should be able to reason the high track to "purpose."

Is it possible for rational organic to assume conscious stewardship of "purpose?" It may not be the drastic sacrifice envisioned. Saturation is preordained and relieves consciousness of mundane managerial duties.

Citizens of the Fifth may diligently pursue utmost command of their interests and maintenance of self and passion, keeping each vital and flexible by fostering recognition of familiarities with all other interests and disciplines. (adapted from Herman Hesse) It is a seeking into the phenomenal not an escape from it.

* This moves realm into more value and creates equity in realm as property. That sounds like a process that will make humanity more valuable to God.

A common contributing corridor of energy with enhanced capacity of contribution, a global fiber-optic nervous system of rational organic and a "new and improved" win/win interaction of ideas and ideals will exponentially cement opportunity for re-investment,……..or not. There were millions and will be untold investment opportunities that have been/will be dissolved at loss and many are actually visible or detectable in the extremely limited cosmos of electro-magnetic spectrum.

Long after untold generations of rational organic, Dark energy will evolve any universe to an un-measurable, far beyond dream.

However, this is when rational organic exists and is the ultimate extrapolation of point in one contributory opportunity of realization. As a successful replicating process in the scheme of perpetuity evolution from point to rational organic has increased embellishment and is occurring more "now" than ever before.

There is a greater "wealth" that exists in every contemporary moment that was not there in preceding civilizations and there are more and more moments. This will simply add up to greater contribution. (quality?)

A scheme with such energy reciprocity may be likely to continue. Assuming that such a scheme be encouraged and that the algorithm continue into the Fifth Civilization of Human kind, the position of rational organic will harbor within a pristine salvation as one of "chosen." A mere four civilizations of patience before "people as a species" are a recognized contributing corridor of energy in perpetuity principle. (rantings of ancient prophets and wise men may be finally realized in the Fifth)

The occurrence of rational organic has a declared meaning and purpose.

Individual moments are different but identity may be maintained by an unchanging, Dark divine sharing,...a tag.

In each corner of each moment this illustrates "possession." Fleeting pulses of spectrum cannot be owned, nor can contribution to Godhead. (no identity) The experience has occurred and is remembered only in the "consciousness being ahead of itself." (of rationality)(motion)

Ralph Waldow Emerson, ...adapted from.... "The Oversoul" (1841)

"Men live in succession, in division, in parts and particles. Meantime within man is soul of the whole, wise silence, universal beauty, to which every part and particle is equally related,...the eternal "one." This deep power in which we exist and whose beautitude is all accessible to us is not only self-sufficing and perfect in every hour, ...but,.....the act of seeing and thing seen, seer and spectacle, subject and object are all one. We see the world piece by piece, but the whole of which these are only shining parts in light energy spectrum,.... is Dark soul."

Suppose that a rational organic of the Fifth has been made aware of, and understands its meaning and purpose. Suppose that it recognizes a divine "tag" that it shares with perpetuity principle and suppose that it "gets" an unchanging ownership of identity within discontinuity and spectrum. Knowing that identity is not forwarded with energy contribution, rational organic may at the "time" of personal "value" be inspired toward maximum aesthetic experience. Understanding scheme of perpetuity principle may be a vivid win/win situation.

It has been said, mostly by practitioners that contribution and reward are obtained in extraordinary experience of occurrence.

In such a situation, where is direction? Perhaps individual direction is the most wanting emotion in existence and there may be a natural urge or tendency to join, or desire belonging. This may be inherent as a self-prescribed method of increasing contribution. From an emotional side, the "feeling" of such interaction may be one of a "link" with an equity providing property,… possession of a relationship such as global membership,…..family affection,…...or even as a fundamental,…..birth itself.

Within a property of rational organic the link of inclusion is a comfort of direction.

It may be more necessary in commonality and not so much so in exemplar individuality.

"In commonality,"…Ralph Waldo Emerson…."The great unity is oversoul within which every man's being is contained and made one with all others."

"In the passionate individual,"….Ralph Waldo Emerson….."The soul answers never by words or understanding but by the thing itself that is inquired after."

In either case or millions of contributors in below, average, or exceptional situations, belonging is absolutely assured in a property of attendance. Dynamics of attention are strivings and resistance to chaos and as such "order" is paramount in all situation as one, or one of the ones.

Aristotle:…."a property is an attribute or quality that is particular to a whole class or species but not its essentiality." Order may be the significant in the property of rational organic just as Dark chaos may be the significant of its essentiality.

In such a situation there may be a portion of Holy Trinity as "method" that is armature of "action." This is gravity wave rent in cosmic extrapolation and trigger that fires critical precinct abundance across pressure membrane and into point.

Adaptation of Itzhak Benton in "Sound Theory."

"There is one great chaos contained in all possible frequency. In this is potentiality for any event phenomena. Vibration resounds in its Dark realm and is infinite interference."

Trigger is hour-glass narrows of Vani, Nadia, Dneipo, Ron and the others of so long ago. Electro-magnetic spectrum is not a priori detectable but must be made so by design limits introduced at point. (with extreme unfolding possibility) Introduction of irritant results in wrapping of layers (hadras) of time. A pearl of wisdom begins with gravity as "method."

Gravitation has been defined simply as "moving in the direction of something." The edge of a chaos maelstrom has an intriguing and encompassing gravitational component. Vacuum energy in state of embellishment forms tensile capacity. Like an inflating balloon, similar energy contributions remain in precinct, creating stress nodules. (quarks have a tensile attraction that keeps them in at least pairs. If separated the tensile quality increases.)

When potential differences occurring across bulbous energy pressure membrane become critical, gravity rent as trigger, as method and as irritant fires abundance into limiting point, a process of investment with no maturity date, but desired result. (of contribution)

In "chosen" corridors such as electro-magnetic spectrum this is rational organic. The introduction of balloon and point is usually always "action."

A cosmological constant of electro-magnetic spectrum is speed of light,.....it is result. Not so easily described is a primary instigator of cause and effect.

"Gate" of a pendulum is necessary in any and all perpetuity principles. An inferred plurality may only be a suggestion of many points opening the creation scheme in many types of bulbous stress nodules that have acquired a critical "buoyancy" and are ready for trigger.

In example of electro-magnetic spectrum, gate may just be gravity induced rent. It is "force that contains by limitation"...not of chaos sea, but of familiar cosmological constants that are released at point. (the constants are clearly visible though not identifying the tree because of the forest is common)

Another perspective of precinct energy module... theories from Heisenberg and Einstein suggest that in a nodule of Dark chaos vacuum energy, vitality is fluctuating constantly and cannot ever be "known" in a scientific or theological way. It may be empty, filling or saturated. This is the "uncertainty principle" and from the point of view of cosmological constant which is situation, it has a time limit. When critically minimal the limit recognizes nodule as seething toward a situation of imminent action.

This quantum uncertainty model is accordingly very accurate and is suggesting an ultimate potentiality of Dark energy that may be "collapsed"

(pin/balloon) (extreme limiting opportunity) into one of endless forms of creation. This is a perturbation theory at its best.

Micro-wave background radiation may be pressure energy membrane. If "coupling" is contribution without identity returning investment to chaos reservoir then "de-coupling" may be action that creates point, a binary situation, a homogenous sub-atomic energy sea clumping into complexity due to gravity wave method. Nuclear furnace cooling to electro-chemical bonding and charge making atomic and molecular activity opportunistic.

(adapted from "Cosmos" by Dana Berry)

Event horizon, microwave background radiation or nodal pressure energy membrane are the threshold or "sill." Tensile expandability may be illustrated almost peripherally in space/time at gravitational lensing. Armature as scaffold supporting method at pin accessing node may be directrix of gravity.

In a cosmic design of energy fabric entangled with a greater then cosmic principle a nodal aspect may be named at intersection of weft.

A hint of process in perpendicular energies interacting at nodal fabric entanglement may be electro-magnetic forces of photon spectrum in familiar cosmic address. Vitality of magnetism and direction of electric current will always be at right angles. In a situation of energy fabric entanglement this is certainly a classic but in all probability, may only be one of the ones.

Tensile pressure may have what may be referred to as a "positive" (in terms of ability to do work) charge. Within a realm (homeostatic) yet uninitiated one may suggest inability to do work and therefore maintenance of a "negative" charge.

The role of an excitable energy pressure membrane field between the two is to support a difference until critical abundance is ripe for investment.

"Quintessence" in an Encarta Dictionary is described as;… "purest most perfect example of something,(being) embodiment, essence, properties in highest concentration, Fifth element."

In an abstract imaginative "push" one may visualize an extremely localized state of polarization at an individual, as in one, point on energy membrane. Gravity the "Quinta essentia" triggers synapse, initiating instantaneous propagation of (in the familiar sense) nuclear energy.

Gravity as an Alpha Helice (neurological analogy) (from Wikipedia)

This S4 is a sensing helix pin-pointing the location where a kind of polarization may occur on the excitable energy pressure membrane. (cosmic background radiation) If the gravity S4 also has a positive charge do to its workability function, repulsion keeps point in closed state.

If location on intersection of energy weft indicates pulses of tensile elasticity the critically taut force of repulsion may rotate Alpha Helice forming/causing helix induction and conformational change such that ionic potential of Dark chaos energy may flow through gravitational limit of familiar frequencies. (such electro-magnetic or sub-particle behavior is evident in quantum hypothesis)

The perpendicular rotation.

When the long axis of a pin is pushed against a balloon nothing happens. (yet both are positively charged) If the pin is caused to be flipped perpendicularily at application point, positive and negative will explode into interaction.

In evoltage, sensitive protein domain S4 is known as paddle, and initiates energy transfer, manipulation and trigger in work process.

Gravity as Alpha Helice acts very similarily in disruption, irritation or perturbation of a homeostatic Dark chaos energy sea.

Suppose that a precinct energy nodule has been manipulated at ripe critical abundance,…. and …..point, with ability for all and any creation is described. Reservoir balloon would de-couple or de-flate and send familiars of which it was saturated into that one type of creation as limited descriptive process with a possibly extendable time frame of investment maturation.

(evolution)

There is a hypothesized cosmological situation describing this situation that has become quite popular. (big bang)

There is another hypothesized cosmological situation as the opposite that has also become quite popular. (black hole)

What if deflated balloon maintains point with critical abundance now on the "other" side of excitable energy pressure membrane? Would creation not want to tumble out of point.

Of course, these two hypothesized cosmological phenomena are well detailed and documented. Are they pin pricks in a localized familiar source of chaos energy rhythmically illustrating the bellows of Boshintoi's eternal perpetually engendered scheme?

So much discussion has been about parallel universes but one might really consider universes at right angles. Perpendicular layering sounds much more functional as an operand.

In divine theory, a creative act or unit of spark, performance may not appear to have stimulus but it is as present and fleeting as peripheral glimpse of movement, a verve with purpose.

It is in recognition of aesthetic experience,….. artistic vitality and vigorous spirit that evolved rational organics within time frame of investment maturation to truly realize energy of "experiential being,"….. that is contribution.

In that robustiousness is a vulgar and crude beauty, a struggle for life from moment of crying out to finality of death rattle.

It need not be corrupt gluttony of a selfish ego or selfless restraint of a wandering yogi. Experience of being may be much easier and more rewarding with wisdom of meaning and purpose. Every situation will make contribution simply in process of occurrence or happening.

Aesthesia may be perception of quintessential "rude awakening." Is there a disgust in arriving in animal form? What about de-animalizing? Is a more refined method of pro-creation on the horizon for rational organic? Would contribution be decreased by vulgarity or enhanced by intellect or spirituality? Every "situation" will contribute.

It is basically granted by theology scholars that God of the three Abrahamic religions are the same God and that Buddhism, Hinduism, Mayan, Hopi or Taoism etc. are all the same God. Perhaps this is because they are all God of rational organic whose presence is derived from and depends on experience of "familiar,"…strong and weak nuclear, gravity and electro-magnetic wave in form of quantized self propagating, oscillatory field disturbance. (from Wikipedia: Gravitational Time Dilation)

On the other side of portal is God, (Dark) reservoir of all creation and energy node that with enough contribution becomes critically stressed and ripe for access by Alpha Helice. In cosmos …gravity and in consciousness,….there is simple belief. It is product of rational organic. It is aesthetic energy of contribution. It does not occur in animal. It is "gravity" of knowing and being known.

Those which are not within boundaries of comprehension are those which are outside of familiar creation and are "different" than chaos reservoir Dark of rational organic. Truth, trust, opinion, value, property equity,…belief is not animal.

This creation has a simple physics. Believing in it and patterns of learning are well defined yet reliance, care, integrity, conformity and compliance are still of animal. Disgust in this blended arrival? One would hope not. De-animalize?….perhaps.

How will belief as gravity Alpha Helice in consciousness reconcile with a clandestine doubt and "pin-point" creation.

Muhammed said:…"at the end of time every soul shall know what it hath produced." Then contribution is complete and so is identity. Creation scheme will always continue, perhaps in familiar or perhaps in "different" precinct energy nodes. Proof is in function of occurrence.

It is one of the plural ones in the one perpetuity principle and has and will continue to "happen." Perpendicular layering sounds functional and so does belief as gravity of consciousness.

An attractive situation of interpretation may be in simple definition. In those criteria that are not animal but rational, belief is that anything or something is a real occurrence,….. when there cannot ever be an absolute proof of validity other than occurrence.

"A partner in dialogue with God is not only individual but human species as a whole." (Gordon Kaufman)

"All occurrence is not only made by God, but of God." (Giordani Bruno)

What of ripples in homeostatic Dark chaos sea that may propagate to a very different, distant alien shore?

When gravity rent opens point to begin a creation it begets occurrence. It is active with purpose like an S4 paddle and in a disturbance or irritance of homogeny there must be a kind of wake. Occurrence is "order" so could a ripple of such traverse chaos?. that from which it was made by limitation,…or not? If so it will be subject to "tracking."

Is a Dark chaos energy sea smooth or rough? If smooth then perhaps, but if violently textured with expanding or contracting, inflating or deflating energy nodal origami,…then probably not.

Situation of familiar occurrence may never be recognized on a very different though perhaps not so distant alien shore.

A citizen of the Fifth will "trust" personal species dialogue, temporal prayer, Dark God realm and valid situation of being as "believable" reality that can only in integrity of "truth," … infer …absolute evidence of condition. It is an end result of rational organic and confident and authentic reality of being. (gravity of belief)

What about this Dark energy chaos homogeny as violently textured entanglement of overlapping perpendicular interwoven vigorous weft?

Sounds positively ripe for a perpetuity principle of unlimited creation. What if Dark chaos storm is so,…. because of a great wind,….. just as in the lower case? As below,…. so above.

"Wind" is an "active" That may bring change within its possible advantage of chaos homogeny. A "further" may forward an influence not only at a possible surface but in a thoroughly penetrating energy sea-scape of saturation.

Can one consider the active that may be influence of storm?

As elusive as a wind, the imagination may need to "push" a little "further."

May it be said that this wind is an active of Dark Matter?

There is a belief that energy is gravitationally drawn to matter. Could this be irritant that causes gravity wave rent in critically buoyant energy nodule? A Holy Trinity that only required a "further" in description of method.

Sand in organic realm creates pearl.
Rationality in animal realm creates time.
Dark matter in Dark energy realm creates universe.

Is it collective imagination or are key phrases like belief, gravity, creation, work, time, active or ripe somehow being brought into better interactive focus by a kind of string that folds over itself to become a "fastening" of sorts? This knot can be equated to a node of universal interwoven overlapping, vigorous, perpendicular energy weft and location of any one of familiar/or not precinct saturations.

An energy membrane which may be heard or seen, as cosmic micro-wave background radiation seems to be where all action occurs. It is not a thin pliable sheet as such but may be better considered as a completely entangled pressure gradient.

It is currently referred to as "relic" radiation and in tradition of short-sighted limited imaginative vision, is considered an ancient or decayed vitality. This kind of idea is a settling point and not operand of the Fifth. Ancient, yes, as in before all time but in vital decay, definitely not.

Without reiterating process of point creation at familiar energy node, "one" may "further" address "wind." As "change" this great wind may be "recurrence of like but not same." (Ibn Arabi)

35

"Dark matter as salt that is dissolved in solution of Dark chaos energy sea, may when coming out of solution be sprinkling the irritant necessary to pin-point locations on energy pressure membrane where gravity rent and point creation can occur."

Perpetuity of such action may depend on momentum. (the secret Fifth force in primary rational carriers)

"Momentum:" (Encarta World Dictionary)...capacity for progressive development, the power to increase at an ever growing rate, a measure of movement expressing purpose and resistance to slowing.

Sounds like there may be an extraordinary "presence" of Dark chaos vitality and dissolved Dark matter that are not being used at energy pressure membrane to forward gravity wave rent and begin a creation.

If percentage of "loop" to violently textured energy homogeny and salting of Dark matter in that sea, is relatively smaller then "momentum," capacity and product of mass and energy in that sea would push eddies of perpetuity principle forward.

Is there a host in monstrance of existence? Yes,... and it may perhaps be described.

Acknowledgement of perpetuity principle is an aesthetic idea and has equity in property of value achievement. Even though hypothesized it may be considered contribution. It has happened and embellishes.

Is this part of the "revealing" of ancient Kaballah, Koran, Talmud, Bagatavistas or Taoism,.....etc. There may indeed be levels of revealing, not increasing levels of complexity but simplifying. It will be the simple things that endure.

So a Dark chaos storm is a roiling energy of turmoil salted with Dark matter. It has a capacity for progressive development and power to increase at an ever-growing rate. It is a measure of movement. This ultimately confused and textured homogeny also carries the multitude of triggers necessary for creations.

Perhaps in a boiling froth of vitality a single, simple grain of Dark matter triggers gravity rent, effecting critically buoyant energy nodule.

(origami because it is "shaped" by familiar energy contribution, scattered throughout storm, and labeled only by pressure gradient membrane) This rent forms point and that attractor has begun a cosmic flow of creation.

(universes)

They may occur everywhere and every-when as maelstrom continues unabated with its own momentum roaring into its own oblivion.

Yet there are doldrums in this fantastic process. There are billions of sun universes created by Dark matter rent that do not evolve into contribution by evolution and worship. They are not as such defeated or ruined but are never figured into "time" and will not embellish. They are not aesthetic and may at best add to creation fodder in supply of fundamental elements.

If a rational organic from familiar energy spectrum has sufficiently evolved and can grasp the magnitude of such creation then they have read through phenomenal and divine dynamics to track that describes purpose.

Such a one in kinship with that one will have no more talk of the Gods of religious dogma.

Having occurred and happened that aesthetic idea is a true beauty held in eye of beholder. It is a favorable quion on which to build the unique experiences of a lifetime.

That involvement is granted in act of sharing that prayer of rationalism brings to altar of awareness. It is reward for contribution of being, repayment of start-up investment and achievement by work moment.

It would be appropriate that Dark chaos energy, Dark salt and momentum are within each moment (and they are as soul) and when moments end they will continue with the perpetuity principle as Holy trinity of further creation.

Just as rationality is end result of creation, be it based upon carbon, silicon or something quite different, so will Dark, salty chaos energy sea be source of creation.

In analogies of type of existence shared by all rational organics since their appearance there is track available. It was there at dawn of humankind and will be there at closing. Dark energy will evolve totality of a universe to an un-measurable.

The most aware civilization of humankind will be that of the Fifth. One might only push deeper into the imaginative before compiling a hand-book of the Fifth.

This violently textured fractal chaos sea had long ago been named by Kongo primitives. They called it "Kalunga" and it was their understanding that it was located between divinity and manifestation. One might "push" that a little "further" to suggest that it creates the divine and manifest. In ritual involvement with Kalunga an ideogram called a Yowa was traced in sand. It symbolically revolved from birth to awareness to transformation to dream-time. In the center was absolute "point" and this was where divinity became phenomenal and the manifest became divine. (adapted from, "Hero with an African Face" Clyde W. Ford)

That might sound like Dark matter/gravity wave rent describing point of creation on energy pressure membrane at origami vitality,..... out/in flow

The Bakongo tribe also named a ritual vessel of enlightenment that one may use to cross that sea. It was a "prenda."

Does the pilgrim of the "high road" access or construct, or perhaps reveal such a receptacle of focus to sail through the hour-glass narrows just barely glimpsing Dark salt energy desert/sea beyond reflection?

This prenda may be a self-constructed revealing.

In one of the most obvious of ancient Carpatian disciple stories one would find Dneipo in his self-constructed revealing, in a traditional dhow (his prenda) crossing the Indian ocean. The extreme depth that he was able to take his revealing, brought him to a realm of a great primordial sea mother. This was where Dneipo was able to entertain sanctum of an open soul. This was as alien as death itself and perhaps the "ancient" that offered this journey intended a sort of visitation to the "other side" of a pressure energy membrane.

His senses were numb yet he could interpret white noise chaos of crossing into extreme pressure. His cognitive map was blank and his rational fragility was temporarily dormant. This was when "Dasein" of Martin Heidegger had nothing more outstanding and was a one wholeness that ignored complexity of work moment. This was fervor of chaos dynamic and the wind that powers its turbulence.

Birth, awareness, transformation and even dream time are at point and his prenda was unerringly sea worthy. Dneipo was able to cast these off and sail into that which creates divinity and experience. He was not able to "know" it, but cried like a baby after returning from it.

A self-constructed revealing of citizen of the Fifth will not be a dhow inching across the humid summer calm. It will be the vessel "Stormbringer" not because it brings storm but because it brings awareness of the perpetual manipulation of "storm."

This is Bonesy whale-riding his myth-beast "Stormbringer" through undulating beta-waves, not alpha helices but the next nearest to them. Even if all is indeed imaginary (as it must be) then contribution is still offered as aesthetic. The greatest embellishing aspect of rationality is imagination.

Dark matter and chaos salt of violently textured turmoil sea of disorder, (containing all order) may be as elusive as its dissolved familiar,.....sea salt. One knows it's there in a super-olfactory aspect, just as one knows ocean scent. In a natural sea situation increased energy causes greater molecular vibration and salt particles manifest as physical environmental phenomena.

Cosmic physicists may know that an allegory is probable. A point will of necessity increase energy yet it is caused by Dark matter/ gravity rent and hence,...... after initiation.

So, what energy will increase in violent sea of disorder to expose Dark matter salt to a phase in which it becomes irritant?

One might have to suggest that in such a maelstrom of energy any increase in vitality may have to arrive from outside of that system.

Gradual, yet relentless contribution from the other side of cosmic background radiation membrane, (that being the side of electro-magnetic spectrum and aesthetic rationalism of carbon based organic, or other) is constant. That embellishment, especially in familiar, nodal, origami energy precincts may be able to desalinate Dark chaos sea as a familiar wave frequency protuberance.

Retrieving Dark salt from this sea would form opportunities of energy attraction (gravity) toward this Dark matter to open gravity wave rent at pressure membrane and form point creation.

Becoming a citizen of the Fifth may mean regarding and intending constant saturated interaction with such ideas.

So,....Dark salt (Dark matter) dissolved in violent Dark chaos energy sea, is with addition of vitality from familiar precinct donors a form of distillation. A purity, an essential aspect or implication of this may be recognition of emergence of irritant that will be wrappings of pearl, time or cosmos. Additional energy will condense brine of chaos sea to reveal Dark matter salt, the granule of which creates gravity and hence rent.

When a system is perpetually successful it develops equity as a value-added property and intimacies of such a scheme may be signaled, marked or tracked for recurrence. This is however still an area of pure discontinuity and any occurrence is of like but not same.

Principle in perpetuity is true constant but result will always be variable. Creation options may "feel" like familiar others but inconsistency of unlimited energy and unlimited salt interaction must form a fluctuating design criterion. Each creation will be an unspecified quantifier that will present an individual circumstance in an eternity of discourse.

A mathematical function that relates "value" of one variable to those of other variables, to constant and to Dark sea is,...one to one. It is a description of plural ones.

Individual may be of an electro-magnetic or light energy spectrum or of something quite different. A rational organic evolved from star dust of familiar energy spectrum may spiritually benefit from acknowledgement and recognition of such a relationship.

It may help to minimalize cosmic gossip and thereby enhance tranquility in miniscule frame of contributory energy event. A gradual yet relentless embellishment emphasized by sheer number and insatiable quest for quantity and quality of experience may be better balanced by a deeper understanding of plural ones. (billions of galaxies)

The moral catch 22 may be that all experience, good or bad, heavenly or evil, intelligent or ignorant and beautiful or ugly are all still aesthetic,.....it is simply relative to commonly held universal gossip.

Reference was to spiritual benefit and that, although of necessarily maintained familiarity must be remembered as a type of non-phenomenal growth. That is active and is a track that has intention of being read.

It may be a situation that allegorically implies the electron of an atom disappearing and reappearing at a higher energy orbit with visible peripheral effects. Spiritual enlightenment spins off quite a variety of peripherals. They often suggest, as in the preaching of Abrahamic prophets that it is a charitable donation to raise currency or "value" of spiritual benefit.

The non-phenomenal growth seems to suggest non-phenomenal reward.

All is probable except for inclusion of identity.

One to one function has been seen in an infinity of situations. It may be as constant as chaos sea vitality and therefore as enduring. It will always be the simple that endure.

Cosmologists agree that Dark matter cannot yet be categorized. A search for this particle is one of major effort in physics. One cannot readily (only with additional energy) find salt in a natural sea even for an extreme searching yet it can be smelled from miles away. Exhaustive manipulation of various proposals may not ever provide a description unless settling points are overcome.

Adapted from Wikipedia essay on Dark matter:

"The instance of Dark matter may have very little in common with "familiar" matter of creation (rational organic) and that elusive universal storm may only interact with a visible universe through gravity."

Again,.....perhaps it is indeed initiator of gravity rent. Anisotropy of distilled Dark salt particle may be simple in critical tensile buoyancy. Particle will come out of solution when there is effect from outside nodule origami precinct. Increased vitality in packet of chaos energy sea describes direction of creation from "signal" via a recipe of similar but not same success. (variable)

Each creation will be an unspecified quantifier emerging from cosmic microwave background radiation. Even in using the phrase anisotropy there is suggestion of a crystalline (properties that are different from different directions) character. Variables that depend on "direction" of instigation.

Salt is such a crystal in familiar situation and Dark salt may occur as a Dark crystal. Familiar markers often "suggest" divine, or greater ideas.

In a familiar realm salt crystals add zest, piquancy (sharply stimulating or provoking) liveliness and vigor.(Encarta)

In a Dark chaos energy realm, Dark crystals distilled from solution would add via gravity rent, all vigor and energy from point to develop zest and provoke stimulation of creation.

In relative quantum field theory of electrodynamics is a description of the way in which matter and energy interact.

It is a perturbation theory of irritation in quantum vacuum at energy membrane of relic radiation.

Also evident in energy deviations and Dark matter halos illustrated in gravity lensing, and at fringes of galaxies, are similarities in a convincing argument for Dark salt as initiator.

Cosmologists and physicists are searching for a sub-atomic particle that even with significant finger pointing may never be found. Perhaps it is a Dark matter salt crystal dissolved in a chaotic Dark energy sea.

When point is initiated an immediate barrage of familiar electro-magnetic (or other) frequencies saturate any form of measurement and "action" of gravity rent is hidden.

"Maco, Eros and Ogle" projects will only show exclusion of candidates for locations of Dark matter.

"Wmap and Plank" projects show that most (probably all) of Dark stuff does not interact with familiar matter or photons except via gravitational effect.

If Dark matter salt crystal is dissolved in Dark chaos energy sea its furtive character would be assured and immediately upon assuming crystalline form it becomes trigger via gravity to tear energy membrane and create point. This activity is again hidden by immediate familiar energy deluge (whatever it will be) as Dark matter salt crystal returns to solution.

To recognise or measure gravity rent would be a situation in which one could look over the edge of an event horizon and beyond basics of space and time. Trajectories of event are discontinuous world-line and may be quite difficult to supersede.

Searching for "activity" of perpetuity principle may be a harness of frustration, however living with knowledge of it may be freedom within light.

Is rational organic still too much animal and are settling points perhaps safe-guards preventing true comprehension? Where in a possible continuing measure of evolution is a rational organic?

Many professionals would say that it is at the top of game. That could be questionable. A mere four civilizations have occurred in twenty thousand odd years of rationality. That being roughly based on emergence of spirituality from the most ancient rock art paintings of "San" people of present day Namibia and tribes of Kalahari.

This is a very, very most recent development of evolution beyond only life and consciousness and just beginning of worship, spiritual benefit and thus contribution.

One might say that perpetuity principle has great patience, but remember that without time, perhaps evolving states may be considered simultaneous and instantaneous. (even the Peso was once de-valued because there were too many zeroes)

The entire lead up to rationality being quaintly arbitrary.

(a constant that is not assigned specific value other than direction)

So,....one might suggest to professionals that only at the Fifth will there be an entry level situation of rational imagination to extend cosmic suggestion and aesthetic value and increase contribution. That is essential of pendular upswing that will ensure appropriate energy devolution via Dark salt incursion (irritant) of chaos sea and hence creation.

Perpetuity principle may be quite simple, enduring by definition and comprehensive involvement of untold and probably unimaginable situations of Holy Trinity activity.

A citizen of the Fifth might swim in Dark chaos sea with a pocket full of Dark salt. A sprinkling here or there may "initialize" (prepare software for use, often by resetting memory location to initial value) This may be a reminder of familiar contribution to precinct nodes of vitality. This "signal" of successful reoccurrence of like but not same may suggest formula of a scheme that has/will mature (evolve) toward rationality and ability to repay investment and contribute.

It may be so simple that a tree cannot be found in complexity of forest, even though one is essence of the other.

Sustainable energy situations will not arrive in any familiarity by complexity.

How does a Tibetan boil water for their tea? ….not including burning dry Yak-dung because that is a precious and very complex process.

Solar energy must activate scheme of a plant based organism with presence of water. As harsh as conditions may be in that high mountain landscape, that life will illustrate growth and attempt action that will ensure reproduction of itself.

Then along comes a Yak and it eats that plant based organism. That must have involved some type of intuitive cognition. Not too many Yaks survive trying to eat rocks. So a Yak demonstrates growth, also in presence of solar warmth (not much) and water, (not much) but that is nature of beast.

A huge line of plant and animal evolution is already present and involved. Assuming that this Yak is not biologically assimilated by a T-rex its digestive system and all of those intricacies will continue to produce Yak poo.

Tibetan herdspersons have learned what has become a bit of a one-sided relationship with Yak. The animal gives them all of their physical resources and herdspersons provide very little in reciprocity. Since T-rex aren't around much anymore one couldn't even suggest protection. So….there is an entire evolutionary scheme and all of those survival and reproductive processes involved in producing Yak poo.

High plateaus and "pastures" of the herd are basically barren, unforgiving and cold so herdspersons loves their warm (good for soul) tea. Will they collect poo and warm their tea or go back to the beginning of evolution?

Well thanks be to the high altitude simple and enduring spiritualism of isolation. They go back, build awesome solar ovens and portable unique focal devices to boil water for their tea with energy directly from a star.

Aside from a fact that the Yak definitely needs representation from animal activist groups one can clearly see a complexity involved in burning Yak poo.

One cannot help but hope that with a pocket of Dark salt and an energy maelstrom, a humble citizen of the Fifth will realize how ancients and Yak herders simplify energy solutions.

There will be a becoming, an energy of self and subject, vitality that is not rigid in electro-magnetic imagination,....open to variables not strict disciplines of a familiar but in a forever, flexibility of creation options from unlimited Dark chaos sea and limited Dark salt.

A Carpatian may need only one goal-line, one end of race. Understanding that salt, as trigger, is "in" chaos begins turning a last corner, and coming down the straight high road to an ultimate identity completion.

Ties with other disciplines will not be easily recognized. In a timeless realm where would they be found. In a fractal point extrapolation how would that be found?....by what?

So,...a search may be a bit of harness of frustration. That's OK because whatever subject or discipline,....it is all still harness of contributory work moment and value of vision and is never directly ahead but always in periphery.

The Large Hadron Collider; (from Wikipedia) was built by Cern between 1998 and 2008 in collaboration with over 10,000 scientists and engineers from over 100 countries as well as hundreds of universities and laboratories.

LHC's computing grid is a world record holder comprising over 170 computing facilities in a global network across 36 countries. One might believe that engineers, particle physicists and cosmologists would argue the complex fundamentals of this relative to any other rational occurrence. Rationality allows this project. It is all aesthetic achievement in work moment. Well into realization of phenomenon at a macro or miniscule level, the "grid" is within a quagmire of complexity.

It is looking for a God particle in the wrong place and it will not be found.

Dark salt instigator of gravity rent within chaos sea is one of simple trinity of ones. That function as true constant is perpetuity principle. The scheme and result are absolutely simple, unlike mega-projects of complex rational organic.

One might boil water for tea with star energy and set sail for distant realms on star energy because simple ideas endure, ...and complex probably do not.

Within an energy brine of variables only precinct cross-weft nodule may be able to "suggest" a recipe for similar creation points. This is rationalizing a "type" of contribution. Four civilizations of an identical "type" of contribution have moved slightly from animal sometimes, but really,...not much. Is it too early?...not the first time?

Astrologers and astronomers of ancient Egyptian realm had to wait for engineering to catch up to the ideas before implementation of influential and manipulative processes directed at a naive populace. This was the same, although in different eras in Mesoamerica and SE Asia.

An ancient method of expressing knowledge and exerting influence was a very large monument. Was that a description of the LHC?

Is there a "type" of energy contribution that is unique to a bubble node, hence critical buoyancy in Dark random chaos storm? If one considers "orders" of contribution then rational organic of carbon based evolution should illustrate/demonstrate a "type" of contribution. Assume that four were significant enough to be "marked" for recurrence of like but not same. The Fifth may prove to be a game changer.

Such an opportunity is that carbon based rational organic harvesting an "experience" of reward in exchange for donation may realize in its equivalency the allegory of an atomic electron "jump."

It may have happened at inheritance of first Pharaoh Kings, hence extraordinary ideas with an attempt at dissipating them into and manipulating common of the era,……. culture. This was done by priests as divinity, with icons and legends and later monumental structures. (quite awe-inspiring for simple people)

In a "jump" a previous position of identifiable energy quotient is no longer available yet that same "indicating posture" simultaneously arrives at a "different" perhaps more intense display.

In an arena of similar, familiar type of contribution what might an embellished carriage of donation reap in reciprocity?

Energy loan from Dark reservoir offers "experience" in exchange for aesthetic donation, yet it is generic,….perhaps good or bad, evil or divine. The vessel of the Fifth might sail upon a principle of abundant, "positive," enduring or aesthetically "pleasing" (relative to rational organic) vitality, that was simply not available in the previous four. (hence war, corruption famine,…..etc.)

An embellished carriage of donation may again reap work moment in a new garden, similar to the one so often referred to in dogma of Abrahamic prophets. It is a sub-conscious joy that this garden is again supplying experience in new highly energetic interpretations. It is beginning a time when those who seek will truly find. (physically in extreme sport and emotionally, spiritually and in the creative imagination by pushing the limits)

New innovations of experience are usually not with complicated apparatus but with simple accessories applied in new methods. As boundaries are expanded so far beyond the dreamer of fourth, or third, the "type" of energy contribution of dreamer of the Fifth will indeed illustrate an elegant carriage of donation.

That type of new familiar vitality captured in nodal knots or precincts and inflated to critical buoyancy will be ripe for interaction with Dark salt. Creation from that gravity rent will be much more "beautiful" then in previous.

Indicators of macro circumstance may exhibit in micro. Divine simplicity is abundant and when extraordinary infatuation with complexity is survived by "freedom within light" a true age of beautitude may reside in the Fifth.

If contribution is enriched life experience, a precinct of new familiar nodal vitality will be enriched and when triggered by Dark salt initiating gravity rent, a resulting creation will be enriched.

Rational organic that "plays" in the accentuated creative imagination will be donating a "type" of uniqueness to chaos reservoir.

There is a new unique vitality to global populace. Population migration as refugee or immigrant, or in the multitude of wars, revolution, armed or domestic conflict and natural disaster relocation, there is a new global life energy evident and it is all contribution. Sleepy colonialized pastoral existence is rapidly disappearing as a human population of an ending fourth is willing to embrace the Fifth.

For four civilizations, the "average" rational organic never traveled very far from home, but now home goes with them and they create a new home and that home is a blend of two. The energy experience of those simple lives has just doubled.

"Nadia gave up the search for home. It was no longer a place but a powerful identity of declared inclusion."

As a solar system tumbles around edge of galaxy there may be a great deal more energy interaction. Rational organic has only documented one other such occurrence and can only speculate,...perhaps in a "long count" ....of others.

"This" rounding may have an inspired "sharing" of enhanced vital experience (perhaps via social media?) of play, describing honest positive aesthetic pleasure.

There may be a new global citizen hopefully aware of an extraordinary "jump" in rationality. If that awareness can occur it may be entry level situation of the Fifth civilization of humankind and the most significant happening of rationality in familiar occurrence.

Adapted from; "Luxor media,"....Josh Garret

The only documentation of a previous galactic rounding may have been the Egyptian emergence of the First civilization of humankind. The ancient name of Egypt was "Kemet" and a significantly wide spread practice of medieval times was developed from "Al-Kemet" as "Alchemy" or "from Egypt" the "Dark land." Practice of alchemy became known as "Dark art" but the origin was probably from that ancient rounding when magic of a great Arcanum was present in abundance.

Lists of alchemists as spiritual seekers in various disciplines of art, science, cosmology, medicine, mathematics and magic are well known.

Beginning at the rounding and spanning four civilizations, some of those citizens of the Fifth might be; …. Thoth, Hermes Trismegistus, Pythagoras, Plato, Aristotle, Jesus, Galileo, Da Vinci, Kepler, Isaac Newton, Napoleon, Richard Feynman and Meesh Koo. In their time they were the sources of new energy contribution allowing great embellishment.

Adaptation of the trinity of the plural one from the "Emerald Tablet:"

"Hence I am called Hermes Trismegistus, having the three parts of the philosophy of the whole, and a "declaration of the purpose of star-point will be revealed."

There were three primes of alchemy:…
-spirit within being
-as above so below
-base matter (Dark salt)

The name "natron" was relative to the third prime as a common tendency for salts to "form solid bodies" or "participants." This sounds like Dark salt coming out of Dark chaos energy brine to present Dark matter as irritant to initiate gravity rent and form point from which any creation may occur.

The Egyptian alchemists at the gate of the First were very good at "paying attention." They were "in attendance." In observation, mapping and measurement their rational intelligence was emerging as a First civilization. They recorded the Nile levels, night sky and social environment and applied that knowledge to everything from crop prediction and hence taxation to afterlife.

One might be certain that they monitored the variables of rational awareness. By season, week or even day the fluctuation in general intelligence, spiritualism and animalism would have varied, just as now at the gate of the Fifth. Many forces then as now would influence from outside of organic.

In belief of early Egyptians awareness of "new" experiences, "first received and then returned energy with/at star point Sirius." It was known as "Great provider" and was recipient of souls.

How similar is that to loan of energy from Dark reservoir via Holy Trinity of perpetuity principle to open star point and creation. Then a period of evolution and maturation to arrive at rationality. Knowing self and place and contributing or embellishing by worship as aesthetic to familiar energy precinct.

If fluctuations of rationality could be measured then there must be methods to maximize this intelligent/non-animal contribution of aesthetic worship to create a diamond of spirituality from base carbon.

Great minds (contributors) previously mentioned may have been made great by such a process, and an objective of the Fifth will be to make that process common.

Tombs of ancients were (not so) cryptically decorated with the "way" or "method." Alchemy of Egypt and later Medieval west was a search for the spiritual diamond/philosopher's stone. Elaborations of middle ages took forms of novels or plays. (Alchemical Wedding of C.R. or a Midsummer Nights dream)

One of the most prevalent attributes of "method" was and must be "attention" ......an act of being focused and acutely aware. When one is in such a state patterns of process of initiation are recognized.....

- in ancient Book of the Dead
- in alchemy of philosopher's stone
- in principles of Quantum

Many schools have tried to forward this idea via analogy and achieved some success however it is always a journey within. This wisdom cannot be taught but must be learned.

A student must find within their own rational spirituality, a temple where a certain shelter from calamity is available. Masons actually used architecture on the outside to protect their ceremonies of inner spiritual growth. Temples must however be "occupied" and that suggests possession and that is ownership,...... of creative soul.

"mne-mon-ic".....-assisting or attempting to assist

-device or location as an aid (temple, formula, rhyme)

"toward remembering that ownership"

Perhaps, similar to previous roundings, a great energy saturation is evident on the eve of the Fifth. It may be causing mobilization of entire peoples and encouraging revolution on almost every front,....politically, spiritually, socially and even scientifically.

Ushering in a utilization of all schools, aids, temples, novels, art, media and magic to open awareness of a beginning of the Fifth civilization and thus assure that a valid direction is forthwith,...should perhaps be of paramount importance.

Mayhem is evidence of an unbridled excitement and frenzy in freedom to act. (within light) It is a euphoria of that "leap of faith" and is reward of those who would push status-quo and agitate equilibrium.

In accordance with ancient, and through various ages of alchemy and magic, this is precise moment when a "pause" is critical. One must not get lost in splendor for it is too intense and quite impractical.

Energy, formula, temple or rhyme will need to be recognized as it becomes manifest in that necessary "attention." Once in "attendance" in the new "home" one will remember ownership and accept responsibility of soul. Contribution is not seasonal, weekly or hourly, it is always "on."

(adapted from "Alchemy in Egypt," Chance Encounter)

Because it is "on" as long as life experience occurs, a certain Castilian phrase comes to mind. "Keep self and subject vital and flexible, and forever recognise interaction with all other creation." (adapted from Joseph Knetch/Herman Hesse)

Energy fabric at point:....like a dew-drop in the forest reflecting all of that creation, but also being reflected in all other dew-drops and creations mirrored a zillion times but not "in" each or any dew-drop.

Reflection is separate but a part of creation and this is what rationality is in carbon based organic humankind. Reflection is not simultaneous with being. An interval is just enough to become aware of self within familiarity and to "worship" as a wonderment of achievement and contribution.

Such an aesthetic within work moment illustrates possession. Answering that call is responsibility of action and that vitality may very well be soul of experience. It "belongs" only to "each." This is why identity can never accompany donation.

Accepting ownership and responsibility of soul is one of the ones on its way toward wholeness of a plural one. It is "Alone with the Alone" of Ibn¢ Arabi and "Dasein" of Martin Heidegger. It is helping to achieve what "it" can ever experience or know because at that cusp, reflection is no longer available.

"Impossibility of finding oneself (reflection) in plural wholeness of one is not in any irrationality of design, nor a limit of cognitive facilty, nor the always inappropriate timely transformation,…but on the basis of possessing and donating that "type" of energy." (Martin Heidegger, adaptation)

Perpetuity principle has fundamental resource and scheme to be more selfish then rational organic. Being/reflection interval is granted as reciprocal arrangement in quantum of action.

Fenyman:…Only three types of energetic activity occur.
Einstein:…..Energy cannot be created or destroyed.

When identity no longer "is" very brief Dark spark of previously identifiable by ownership contribution, is obscured in a great turmoil, the roiling Dark storm of Dark chaos sea. A powerful smell of Dark salt is omnipresent and creation possibilities blink past ad-infinitum.

In such a truly indescribable imaginative speculation one and many might ask,….is it animal having spiritual knowledge, or spiritual entity having human experience?

That would not be a question of a citizen of the Fifth. Dark realm is not spiritual knowledge, nor is point creation experience.

These are cause and effect far "pre-moved" of a much later in maturation/evolution rational organics animal spiritualism. At moment of self-realization an aesthetic contribution likened to worship, begins to recharge familiar energy precinct in Dark chaos energy sea. "Location" is not even remotely similar to concept in rational logic.

Like Dark salt it is dissolved,…with access….in chaos maelstrom.

All order, formula, temple or rhyme are dissolved…with access… in Dark chaos.

All Pythagorean, Aristotelian, Rosicrucian, Masonic, Abrahamic, Hindu or even Golden Dawn ideas are dissolved…with access… in Dark chaos.

All completely alien, indescribable, imaginative speculation is dissolved…with access….in Dark chaos.

As such, in this Dark realm there is no spiritual knowledge. Point creation is not experience. It is pin hole gravity rent created by Dark salt as irritant in violently confused homeostatic energy storm. "When" it occurs "previous" supplied precinct energy nodes dissolved in Dark solution are approached with investment opportunity for a formula of proven similar reciprocal contribution.

Are the chosen ones of brief Dark spark of identifiable by ownership contribution part of experience of point creation? Certainly not in direct initiation but probably in anticipated result.

Consequence of point creation may be an entity or order capable of aesthetic energy contribution.

This is purpose of gravity rent.

Purpose of such an order is worship as achievement in embellishment.

Purpose of Dark chaos is unlimited reservoir of creation possibility.

That is purpose of Holy Trinity as perpetuity principle.

Spiritualism in rational organic is recognition of Dark spark within,… and desire to name or describe it. Most human contribution has reached obvious settling points. That is not situation of a citizen of the Fifth.

Owning responsibility of soul involves "pushing" beyond those super easy imaginative stories originally created for much "simpler" people.

Adapted from "the Divine Matrix"…Greg Braden

Rational organic resides in temple of self, the home of a powerful and complete identity of declared inclusion.

This is an energy bridge between chaos energy and contribution, Dark and light. Rational organic is work moment of being, reflecting its own creation,… and,…. an artist expressing realization on quantum canvas.

That is aesthetic in responsibility of active participation and vitality of soul fulfilling experience that is a known and understood contribution.

That would be common practice of a citizen of the Fifth.

As above, so below, yet all indicators of divinity (connected via worship with service of creation) are available on all levels, especially those most common. The "seek and ye shall find" is a truism across cosmos. It may be a discovery by anemnasis, intuition, intelligence and or inspiration,…perhaps a creation and sustainability through a timeless billion years until "time," if and when work moment reappears and pay-back begins. In occurrence of experience all indicators of divine scheme are and must be available.

In order to truly live freely within light knowing and understanding Dark removes fearing it. Realizing unfettered energy contribution and re-investment via perpetuity principle grants a sort of immortality. (though without identity)

Subjective nature of contribution is only relative to human citizenry but when energy embellishment is aesthetically "pleasing" more of such will be identified in reservoir and following creations will necessarily receive "positively" imbued investment.

It may be early to suggest, but four civilizations of antagonism, (as well as the usual definition, one might consider "neutralizing interaction") have perhaps been enough for a maturing rational organic.

Subjectivity has and always will occur in rationality yet is it possible or even probable that it may begin to lean toward a more altruistic function?

(with self composer, attention and "home" in mind)

"This is different from religious dogma,….struggling institutions of preserving ideas of apparent residency."

"This is finally accepting "personal" responsibility of soul."

"Connection via aesthetic worship with service of creation."

"Neutralizing interaction," …..secondary definition of "antagonism" may be wheel block that need be removed in order to roll into the Fifth.

Let rational organic not fulfill the prophesy of film noir "Idiocracy."

Let settling points be moved aside of a work moment of momentum on straight high road.

Let interaction be not nullified but exemplified in "self and subject" vital necessity of ties with all other creation.

Let animal be guided into that which no longer has prevalent animal characteristics.

For only after a clear indication of such, with spiritual riches and an emotionally/intelligent fulfillment, would any creation reveal and allow themselves to again be seen without any clothes. (like the first garden)

Hence a necessity of introducing a civilization of the "Fifth,"….or perhaps not,…there is no relative consequence.

Yet there may be that super subtle suggestion that an aesthetically "pleasing" contribution may instill "pleasing" energy into vast, Dark, chaos reservoir storm of possibility. (still sounds subjective but….)

Adapted from Thomas Moore:…..."Enter Darkness with all strength of intelligent emotion and perhaps find a new vision and deeper sense of self. Do not solve its factual equation but be enriched by knowing it."

Within Dark soul is a power of transformation.

Like an alchemical quoin one must enter understanding and recognize Dark salt in macro as cornerstone of creation and in micro as hall monitor and mentor as Dark soul.

Movement toward chaos is a movement away from order. It is a surrender of controlling aspects of identity and forum, and heightening of "attention," listening not for collective self but for individual soul. Such awareness alters self for the remainder of being. With an ability to delve ever deeper into possibility it is no surprise that the Velikovsky's create such heresy. (Worlds in Collision) (definitely a citizen of the Fifth)

Adapted from "The Oversoul" Ralph Waldo Emerson;……"Soul answers never by words or understanding, but by the idea itself that is inquired after."

It is spiritual response beginning at edge of familiar and going beyond extent of imagination. If realm of civilizations has basically been a coarse, animal or primitive value, then perhaps the Fifth will suggest a quality of refinement, sensitivities and evolution similar to the beginning of the First.

Dark realm is at the well-known interval of light and with that of course,.....it is quite subtle. A loud exuberant presence would not be recommended to a citizen of the Fifth. That is a diametric.

Comfort,...why not. Drama,....definitely not. Heroism,....within subtlety. Worship,...as sharing,.....karma,..... confidence.

Incubation; (Encarta world dictionary) "to develop while being kept in a favorable environment."

Truly unique in evolution of rational organic is citizen of the Fifth. They will accept possibility and responsibility to "attend" to an incubation of soul. Contribution will involve taking "possession" of "home" being in the vital flexibility of all creation and in forwarding a "pleasing" reputation of embellishment.

Dark extends personal invitation to mature spiritually rational being as a worshiper in full measure of its capacity. Not upon settling points but as prayer of Dark god aspiring to issue forth and prayer of being seeking within Dark,... for soul,.......by soul. (adapted from Ibn¢ Arabi)

Every single soul in familiar spectrum has this moment. It is ownership in aesthetics and thus aesthetic contribution. "Dark" of it is absolutely unique, with presence unaltered in all realms. There is a saying that speed of light is ultimate constant but that is subjective, relative and result.

Dark chaos sea as ultimate reservoir contains all formula, temple and rhyme. (the only apparently constant variation may be creation) With gravity-wave-rent trigger and point function trilogy of perpetuity principle is an engendering, continuous, enablement as true constant.

Without possibility of imagining Dark storm or giving it shape, or being aware that even location is dissolved with access, one might struggle with direction. The sea is amorphous and may only be known peripherally beyond a brief reflection at hour-glass narrows as one passes through identity.

It is like a malady of migraine vision. Searching eye for abnormality is futile because irregularity of light and focus is in rationality, manifested as distorted vision.

Searching in rationality for abnormality of Dark in irregular light and focus is futile because it is in soul, unmanifest even as distortion, but in simplicity constant in a plural oneness of soul.

Task of approaching a search on high road has not been presented to human, but to humanity, …..not rational organic but rationality. Only by leaving technique behind can "seeker" be graced with a "finding."

Epic story and myth have survived ages, not fully understood on page, or wall or in monument but allegorically intended as symbolic spiritual directive for "heart,"…home of soul. Stories abound across cultures spanning civilizations and a message pried from imagination has often inferred a "magical" insight. It may be a bringing "fuzzy" (logic) awareness to rationality, yet as a search by soul for soul.

"Magic" presents impossibility, yet function of it can be recognized in possibility. "Magic" as a Dark art may infer Dark insight and though it is impossible to present it in rationality, function of it may be recognized in possibility.

Rationality as aesthetic contributor cannot be used as a tool to unveil Dark chaos. (a can opener supplied in every can) Voyage of Dark passage must be made in ones "prenda" (vessel and possession of enlightenment) utilizing way of soul that is made and carried by same incredible vitality that surpasses "identity of being" so easily.

As vessel is a miniscule containment of that awesome Dark flux, the mere idea of captivity suggests an obligation to "pay attention,"… as soul is so very personally powerful. It arrives as fractal extrapolation of Dark creation womb and returns to it in short order. In brevity of the work moment situation and through all the clamor of that phenomenal dynamic only soul will suggest a wisdom learned as oneness and unity become complex and diverse and then return, having never really departed, to an unveiled divinity.

Those who are willing to seek may not be graced with finding unless they are focused upon high passage. A shallow search may encounter reefs or even mountains on which to be grounded.

Deeper being treads water on a thin perpendicular, rotated, interwoven pressure membrane between Dark chaos storm of all its possibility and identity of its rationality.

Deeper being receives enrichment of individual soul by unified soul and grants an embellishment of unified soul by aesthetic rationality of knowing individual soul.

It is reciprocity carried out by perpetuity principle. A citizen of the Fifth will return, or perhaps never even drift away from a childhood imagination of "magic." They will be receptively humbled in myth of transformation, Dark in such a subtle arrival and to be sure equally elusive departure.

Transformation having barely occurred.

Time has been described as fractal extrapolation and soul has been described as arriving as fractal extrapolation. Rationality contributes aesthetic energy by acknowledging worship. It is in offer of being that Dark essential essence may be recognized in microcosm and inferred in macrocosm.

It is the many who will know that presence and settle with it. It is the few (until a great revelation of the Fifth) who will seek much further.

Coincidence in arrival of time and soul as forwarded in analysis, dogma and gossip, continue to suggest "sharing" within a vessel of containment. Without surprise, this may be rationality and structure and function of such as is in "attendance."

That obligation surpasses the great animal system and is offered in order to do so. A rational is meant or designed for aesthetic growth (hence contribution) and for that a "time of soul" has been given.

Soul is Dark key on inside of a brilliant, almost blinding door in an equally radiant containment of being. Key is made of same "stuff" that is outside. It is a reminder of that which is outside.

Definitions of "key." (Encarta World Dictionary)
- way or means of achievement

- critical aspect that if understood provides knowledge of
   whole
- strategically vital in access
- main tonal center of composition
- mood, style or armature of aesthetic
- cryptographic feature of encoded mechanism

Soul is Dark, chaotic maelstrom of infinitely complex sea within manner of rational containment as order. It is means of achievement and critical aspect of apprehending an idea of energy homogeny. Soul is strategically located with rationality at tonal center of life song. It is framework of life sculpture and secret key of rational evolution.

It may be possessed with rational unit at work moment, yet is a wild tempest of divinity. Wholeness and oneness of it as fractal extrapolation does not mean here or there, but here and there,...then or now, but then and now,... happy or sad, but happy and sad,......kind or mean, but kind and mean,...... and in that unity is volatile aesthetic.

Diversity and complexity suggest calamity that when pattern harnessed denotes intelligence. Serene storm of homogenous Dark chaos sea when neither patterned nor harnessed denotes wisdom. It is wisdom of knowing that every/all formula, temple and rhyme are contained in that Dark corner of rationality called soul and that contribution of being is continually enhancing the macro-infinite reservoir via its key, a strategically accessing cryptograph of pure random chaos held in the micro-essential Dark.

It is way or means of achievement in perpetuity principle for ever and ever? (without identity) therefore accepting responsibility of type, or kind, or aesthetic of embellishment.

An obligation to attend and coincidence of time and soul are prime directives "separating" rational organic from great animal system.

Rational organic has pattern harnessed work moment from calamity intelligently in the previous Four. Perhaps design aspect for aesthetic "growth" may now emerge knowing that "time" will be given and seeking within soul by soul will present a greater then radiant, confident Dark serene finding.

Adapted from: "Dark Night of the Soul" by Thomas Moore

"Following the ancient tradition of Black Sun, imagine a Black Sun at personal core, a Dark luminosity that is less innocent and more interesting then naïve sunshine. That is one of the gifts of Dark night."

"Imagine Dark chaos energy at rational core, an unknowable raging shadow only barely evident in interval of familiar energy frequency spectrum. Such a magical imagination suggests myth of transformation where fractal extrapolation occurs and may be a gift of Dark rich soul.

Behold the Trinity bringing gifts to citizen of the Fifth under ancient tradition of Dark Sun.

Acceptance in rational identity may be a "settling" relative to possibilities held in chaos reservoir,…. accessible by soul.

Previous Four:….pattern harnessed intelligent identity

Fifth:….personal responsibility for chaos of possibility

Beginning for all citizens is alchemical substratum of promise, preparation and performance. Dark magic suggests the wedding of Kaballistic pillars and marriage of sufi-gnostic hadras of determination.

In each case there is a "reflection of correspondence." Image/imagination of track sharing intends reading. Vitality, soul and desire must be made audible in a great symphony of noise.

"Personal responsibility for chaos of possibility," does not suggest mayhem but perhaps an option beyond manipulative culture.

Once entering the Fifth (at any age) it is not listening for essence of promise, preparation and performance, for they will not voluntarily isolate from chaos,…but it is pushing and elbowing into Dark possibility.

"At the end of time," said Mohammad, "every soul shall know what it hath produced."

Shallow souls create shallow dreams that create shallow being and that is lesser contribution and may create shallow reservoir of possibility.

It is still contributory, but a fraction of what is possible. There have been a few noteworthy examples of dominion and a multitude of those unknown,…. but the Fifth will be populated by individual, tribal, cultural, national, and global souls at depth.

"Passage" by definition does not involve waiting or listening. It is corridor, path, a piece of writing, speech or art, change and approval or perhaps a way or means of directive or action. (aesthetics) (from Encarta)

Growth may be as linear as a tree or as nonlinear as a caterpillar changing into a butterfly, but it/they do leave track in homogeny. Such different concepts using the same vocabulary. One may assume evolution of rational scheme,…. just barely out of great animal system,….. and time,… in becoming of passage toward Fifth.

Just as medieval alchemy involved stages and Kaballistic pillars and sufi-gnostic hadras involved levels, so may a citizen move through their passage in phases.

Dneipo passed into Darkness in the mouth of the great Sea Mother. He was introduced but not allowed to linger. That is part of "method" and must be so in "order" to maintain identity and be able to continue, reassured toward Fifth. There are so many similar stories, fables and myths throughout history, religion and antiquity.

A history of a multitude of cultures describe rites of passage that may be shocking, frightening, disturbing, very difficult and always dramatic. In many cases these are near death encounters.

Any shaman must undergo such a passage and sorcerers, witches, medicine men or those who deal with "magical" concepts,….are most obvious. It is referred to as descending into Dark art but perhaps one might re-infer process as deeper insight into Dark soul.

Ascending and descending have that linear inference of tree growth while a shamanic-like rite of passage of citizen has great drama of change from one sense of being to another. This is more like growth of a caterpillar changing into butterfly, or an electron "jumping" to a new higher energy orbit in an atom, …….or any such magical transformation.

Kiijay's transformation was so dramatic that he eventually lost his sorcerer's identity and simply became "Magik." A citizen of the Fifth will be seeking levels, stages and phases that mark growth. Rite of passage may occur in relatively equal doses or as a cataclysmic event that is barely survived.

The finding is: - at interval of energetic order

- emerging from cocoon
- crawling through Dark tunnel
- turning Dark key
- passing ritual
- marriage with deeper Hadras
- advancing soul journey

It is certainly not meant to be comfortable or secure but is a going out on a limb of the tree of life and taking a leap of faith.

Why would one seek such a philosophy? The answer may be evident with the so few who have undertaken it. It is a request by soul for a deeper mark that cannot be ignored. These are remembered names, perhaps of the Homeric path whose Dark soul contribution was great,…. though privilege was moderate. Without seeking wealth or fame their work moment was maximized.

A modern might be somewhat more anxious about reward. Media and social media make desire instantaneously obvious.

Does anyone remember chronology and kairology? One is "time" and the other "timing." After four civilizations of unrelenting movement into future perhaps citizen will allow time to move over themselves, thereby choosing when to "move" and "grow." Rather than pushing toward perceived intention, actuality of passage will arrive forth-with,… perhaps leaving track,…diversion from equilibrium,….and into growth.

Citizen is hero of being not mere observer of passage. Theirs is re-birth in reading their great dream correctly and not "settling" until that which has left dream is unveiled.

Kairology is therefore their significant tool. Four civilizations of being born too soon. Quick,…out of womb,…..what's next? (if each item on a "bucket list" is searched for inspirationally, then valid, but if not that "time" might be better spent) A common coming of age ritual, rite of passage may be re-instated in the Fifth. Hopefully it will re-figure a blind charge into adulthood and "further," a maturity.

Primitive necessity is not yet out of animal but is there striving? A primary phase of Dark energy infusion may be opening of cocoon.

Keats:…"call the world, if you please,….the veil of soul."

A citizen of the Fifth is surrounded by those who are striving but like each of them, they must do it alone. Method, formula or rhyme that is being is personal and can never be taught or purchased. Priests, councilors, even concerned friends or gurus cannot authentically help.

The minute Dark of soul into which one must seek is undisciplined chaos realm in fractal extrapolation of unfathomable chaos sea holding all pattern order and possibility. Caution is not to tap into a great reservoir directly, not while maintaining identity. Structure of rationality is in direct resistance.

The "himma" of Ibn¢ Arabi is heart energy of spirit that is able to approach Dark singularity, just as "Stormringer" did. Vessel (prenda) as possession of enlightenment was aptly named as it carried seekers to the very edge of nuclear furnace. (point creation)

Quote from "Carpadia;"..."just before passing through a star and dispursing into quantum chaos Stormbringer pulled into the fragile sanctity of a cove. It had identity. It was Ttsaa'ahl."

"Himma" of Sufi mysticism is able to strain possibilities from deeper hadras toward limits of order and manifestation. This was how Bonesy and the Poet recreated the Grand Portage used by their ancestors on their way to Holoflux for the Fifth birthday party. It did not intersect with any civilization and they wanted to "remain in the essential" until presentation. They were of course already living in the Fifth.

Nadia and Vani had their cabin in the Tatras.
Ron and Kathy had their cabin with Mr. Racoon at Mendocino.
Henry David Thoreau had his at Walden Pond.

These were cocoons, temples and locations of rite of passage. They were physical places but moreso were places of heart where himma could do work. Whether associated with geographic or physical structure or hiding openly in a structure of psyche, retreat cannot be accessed in the middle of modern calamity.

It may be that truly, there is no wisdom in a phone or laptop, yet wisdom is always with a citizen of the Fifth. It glows at the cabin at a rite of passage and at the metamorphosis. It is change, knowing that all is changed and changing,...... and that it is indication of growth.

Nadia,Vani, Ron, Kathy, Bonesy, The Poet, KiiJay and all the others had many metamorphosis's. They were creating the Fifth even as they were first citizens of the introduction of the Fifth.

In seeking and witnessing arrival of Carpadia, savior of humankind, the Fifth civilization had begun. They had "set the mood" for an eon of greatly enhanced aesthetic contribution.

Perhaps events such as this have occurred at each Galaxian rounding in the maturing, evolving process all the way back to point function, when Dark salt caused gravity rent to occur in chaos reservoir storm and create.

Rationality as end state is contributor of energy embellishment and perhaps similar to levels, hadras or stages of Kaballah, the Fifth is lifting another veil in realizing responsibility of soul and the new variance in the, "address of awareness."

Throughout ancient and relative revelation in theme of spirit, alchemy or science, responsibility had/has always appeared and "sustained" "breakthrough" that is necessary for growth.

It is situation of hero/heroin embracing rite of passage.

(moral, mortal or emotionally intelligent) They have nudged a great singular soul and fantastic forces of absolute chaos and possibility and as ancient Sufi-monks maintained, returned to a participatory realm to bestow a wise treasure upon their fellow humble beings. (Dneipo and Sea Mother)

When citizen is aware of "moment value" they will not be concerned with time,...but timing.

They would not proceed through dream but by unveiling it, dream is allowed to blanket dreamer. Divine Dark vision was/is always within heart energy of spirit in a tiny unaltered corner of soul.

Adapted from St. Symeon:... "the one who has become plural remains the one undivided."

When experiences of living freely within familiar energy spectrum are worn as a blanket,.... opportunity, chance, qualitative aesthetic factors and auspicious moments abound everywhere. A citizen will choose rather than react. Contribution becomes more rich and thorough and as such embellishment of reservoir becomes qualitatively "thicker."

Perpetuity principle does its thing and new creation begins with opportunity for greater beauty and less strife. This is function of the Fifth as enhancing the enhancement again occurs. Phenomenal realm of rational organic tumbles around the edge of a galaxian cosmos.

What happens when a caterpillar changes into a butterfly? This process actually sounds very similar to a shamanic or alchemical rite of passage. It involves digesting self and re-formulating a different presence from its own essential soup.

"Nigredo" (medieval Black crow and Haida Raven) is a part, stage or level of metamorphosis in an alchemical process of marriage, the moving of one state of being to another. (The Alchemical wedding of C.R.)

Polarities, opposites and dualism of seeker are dissolved into each other's essence and a new synthesis is recognizable as one unity. Macro spiritually unique oneness of unlimited chaos sea,.... visible and respected in micro,... Dark of soul.

This is a stillness within citizen (temple) not associated with complexity or diversity. It is a quiet center within which deep aesthetic "beautitudes" can be forwarded from knowledge of that volatile primal.

Although possibly inferred, key itself does not turn. (it is part of Dark constant) Tumblers may and in case of citizen "will" rotate around strategically vital soul. A seeker of high road to true rite of passage will allow that, though it will involve "Dhikr." (recollection, mindfulness and attention) Allowing is deep. It is a liminal position of choice. It may not be comfortable.

Soul will hold to Dark unity. Complexities and diversion of being in ordered state will relentlessly spin and spiral throughout senses, emotions and fears.

It is rationality that receives and carries experience and in that aesthetic is vital contribution to soul. Allowing tumblers of manifestation to rotate is in fact getting out of the way of unlocking new and perhaps radical opportunity of possibility. If any bits of perceived reality are stubbornly seized,.... the door will not open.

Though constantly in process the art of being has been nearly stagnant for four civilizations with very few well-known exceptions. What if all citizens recognized their Dark way beyond the face of God and holding to that soul unity aspired to achievement and accomplishment of those exemplary names of Homeric path?

Contribution will be very thick and it will be for every reason that existence occurs. With a type of "quality" of reservoir storm enhanced, any new creation will "begin" with opportunity for greater beauty.

One might not want to remove reward from self to put it in a heavenly place. Contribution toward and surpassing heavenly realm is within soul already. By continually enhancing the enhancement there is no limit to aesthetic creation,.....it is far beyond any limit of heaven.

Do to function of perpetuity principle the entire process of creation, contribution and re-creation from different energy characteristics will/ must become more and more sublime. (as in a philosophy of aesthetic value) Beauty to a familiar rational organic may be quite different from that of a completely alien contributor yet they both embellish in achievement and enhance reservoir.

How interesting might a creation that arrives from that blend be? That being will also be supplying their own absolutely unique aesthetic vitality to Dark chaos sea.

As may be becoming increasingly obvious, contemporary ideas of heaven and hell are mere unimaginative tactics of dealing with populations of followers. Dogma was designed for simple, barely rational progeny of sheep-like believers in an age of near ignorance.

Metamorphosis of seeker becoming citizen and realizing Dark divine soul of self and sea has been called "gnosis." Direction of this journey with vessel of intent and integrity will navigate an essential soup toward great "beautitudes" and in doing so will "awaken." A great strength that becomes evident in identity has been named a gnostic authority.

"Beatitude" (Encarta World Dictionary) - the perfect happiness and inner peace supposed to be enjoyed in heaven.

"Beautitude" - the continually enhanced gate of chaos caldron of possibility,… forever enriched by aesthetic donation,…..beyond awe, worth and excellence and in that process, absolutely complete in function without beginning or end.

How might one sustain integrity while diverse phenomenal tumblers spin recklessly around soul key? After all, the daze of daylight-slumber is nurtured by complexity. Position is that of reaction (the easier) not choice (the more difficult) and that is not freedom.

Vigilance and vitality are field markers suggesting progress toward a goal of active attention. Maintain completeness, do not allow damage in fragmented field energy and an end line of unified understanding may be accomplished.

Process is completely beyond self-interest. It will be absolutely fantastic when self has awareness of contribution and though rationality is awareness of self, it is also vehicle of contribution.

When experiences of living freely within familiar energy spectrum are worn as a blanket,…..opportunity, chance, qualitative aesthetic factors and auspicious moment are in abundance. Knowledge, wisdom, ability and desire will direct a citizen in "privilege of choice."

Uninitiated seekers may rush over a horizon while citizens of the Fifth may just let it wash over themselves. Time will always bring a multitude option of experience to seekers and in privilege, a citizen will choose their contribution accordingly.

Mohammed:…"At the end of time every soul shall know what it hath contributed." Perhaps at end of time of organic,….. harboring soul.

Well-spoken and quoted on numerous occasions but one might remember that contribution does not bring identity to reservoir.

There may be a suggestion that Dark soul of rational organic never left unified Dark soul chaos reservoir and as such does not "return" with contribution. As fractal extrapolation into "being" it is minute, but not different from chaos storm and that would suggest a constant. Creations are the variable investment opportunities designed to mature into achievement.

Rationalities of perhaps many "types" continually "return" energy to perpetual scheme. Holy Trinity of reservoir, Dark salt and gravity wave rent are active principle as renewable eternal vitality of possibility. This may not be un-directional even though arriving from a turbulent Dark maelstrom. First consideration may suggest a cyclic idea (re-incarnation) but it is via aesthetic donation (without identity) that growth leaves track that can be "read" as worth on markers of high road seeking "beautitude."

"Forever enriched" suggests presence of track and although beautitude is beyond awe and excellence and in sublime realm, a most innocent, humble modest citizen should still be able to accept the idea of absolute completeness. (including embellishment)

Purpose of such an engine would not be to increase completeness but perhaps to be active in drawing attention to quality,......hence aesthetic.

If an old adage is valid and…."energy cannot be created or destroyed"…. any purpose of function would have to be qualitative.

"Perpetuity principle and position of rational organic within it suggest exactly such a situation of embellishment without volume. Human lifespan is very minute and when energy investment for experience is returned by worship only quality of this vitality is different.

Animal cannot create more energy but Dark unchanging soul can monitor rationality and verify aesthetic contribution.

Dark soul fractally extrapolating into identity and then remaining as chaos reservoir after identity,….. brings nothing in either direction, but in process Dark corner is enriched by experiencing a "vehicle" of rationality.

"Beautitude"….The continually enhanced gate of chaos caldron of possibility. Forever enriched by aesthetic donation, beyond awe, worth and excellence and in that process, absolutely complete in function without beginning or end.

A citizen of the Fifth that is able to nudge up against this idea of absolute singularity and comprehend their role in that perpetuity will know a total, yet very subtle, emotional, intelligent and spiritual catharsis. Releasing calamity of spinning phenomenal tumblers may allow a gentle settling around soul key, unlocking the great obvious for some, or maybe only a click or two away for others.

Wrapped in a blanket of opportunity, chance, qualitative aesthetic factor and auspicious moment brings recognition of abundance.

Adapted from......"The Life Codes"..... Patty Harpenau

"Becoming adept at choosing manifestation of being involves tuning ones soul frequency to that of abundance. When deepest heart's desire becomes aligned with oscillations of possibility an interwoven energy matrix will direct a citizen in "privilege of choice." Stepping into a field of limitless possibility becomes less daunting when a purging of debris-baggage of being, a slowing of phenomenal mayhem and warmth of a security blanket have created that "fuzzy quantum-logic feeling." An artist creates on quantum canvas.

"Once upon a time."

With passion, desire, conviction and grace moving ahead and yielding vulnerability to such a fantastic penetrating involvement, a darwish (sill) of creation gateway is crossed. It is empowerment of "first cause" in time realm and like Bonesy and The Poet, a citizen may "choose" to create manifestation.

Creative possibilities of expression will appear before citizen and they must accept permission and responsibility to engage and usher them into foundation of being. Fulfillment will be necessary consequence.

"Being" a citizen of the Fifth might be similar to the Castilians of "Glass Bead Game" by Herman Hesse.

They shall obtain utmost influence of creative process and passion.

They shall keep creative process vital and flexible in relation to all other creative process. (adapted)

Work moment is aesthetic contribution. A sage who has accepted wisdom of the "Great Beautitudes" will/must manifest the sublime.

Snail's pace as it is in time line of rational organic, it is a cosmic blink in discipline of perpetuity principle.

Soul within recognized being is a fractal of Dark chaos sea capable of repeated subdivision into fragments, each of which is a miniscule copy of the whole,...therefore not different from. Rationally individual in identity but energetically undifferentiated via soul, the citizen imagines and experiences absolute epiphany "available" to its form, or "type of stardust."

There may be direction in beautitude. Continually enhanced gate and forever enriched may suggest a maintenance variable but energy loan from chaos energy reservoir of possibility, hints at presence of a huge vault including securing an insurance that is never manipulated.

Miniscule point creation at gravity rent is loan that if matured sufficiently to aesthetic contribution and worship will bring a percentage of quality enhancement via experience of being,….slipped into said vault and thus changing its vitality. That would be "direction" beyond maintenance.

In a scheme that involves absolute completeness "direction" within must be justifiably included. That offers track and the extremely astute citizen may be able to "read" that track, not following toward the "magik" of it, but in an opposite direction, toward that which has suggested it.

Adapted from "Dark Night of the Soul" by Thomas Moore. This author speaks of Dark chaos in terms of forge and smith.

"Dark within is crucible of a forge. Experience of being is manipulated and impressed upon soul. Anvil is altar where that spiritual alchemy forwards raw essential of possibility into manifestation."

At cusp of familiar spectrum only "spark" (perhaps of Jesus) of point creation at gravity rent becomes visible. This is where KiiJay becomes "magik" and creations occur. Stuff of being becomes beautiful contribution and yet,…….. moment itself is just barely out of animal.

A smith is in soul working possibility into shape,….from forge and onto anvil each setting allows "work."

Work moment is tough and basic and it is aesthetic and full of beauty. Direction of beautitude is included in absolute completeness because creation and re-creation from continually enhanced reservoir is continuous within completeness.

Aesthetic of work moment is recognized by Dark soul, a divinity present when rationality arrives. It is self-awareness and belief in identity.

One might move gracefully into moment or allow moment to gracefully blanket…….. attacking work moment is not recommended.

KiiJay, Meesh, Hermes, Bacon and others of Homeric path become "magik" and creations occur.

As fractal extrapolation of Dark chaos sea of possibility,….soul is nourished by beauty. All of being, phenomenal, intelligent, emotional, spiritual and imaginative must be alert and attentive in creating manifestation, as that process possesses the deep-seated vitality that is responsibility of presentation.

Beauty is everything that its colloquial definition infers yet it also includes war, pathos, destruction, fear, misfortune and failure. These,…. all together are the contours of harness or yoke in influencing direction of work moment. It is raw, rough and yet quite "natural" as a process of evolution in environment. Rational organic wears it, same as a plough horse, but with less direct influence of guidance. A plough horse is in a position of lesser "responsibility." It is outfitted and guided by a higher power.

A sufficiently evolved contributing soul-heavy rational organic has no such guidance. "Higher power" is within and fitting is done "during" the activity of being.

Expression is beauty of experience. With rationality, it is specific and explicit. Dark soul as holder of equity in property of experience is direct personal gateway to possibility realm. One must be careful how they wear a yoke of work moment experience. Energy realm is not picky or judgmental regarding subjectively positive or negative donation, for both are aesthetic.

(even the "force" has a Dark side)

Harness might subtly adjust shape to better fit psyche, emotional intelligence or spiritual work station of expression,….and that will effect direction of achievement and ultimately beautitude process.

Ibn¢ Arabi suggested being very aware of true heart's desire,….it is singular possession as one of the ones and is never shared. Heart's desire will create the beauty of an experience,…be it this or that.

One of the greatest Biblical/psycho-analytical quotes applies directly,….."know thyself."

Ideas may become more evident with allegoric image. Perhaps entertain an hour glass narrows of soul between eternal reservoirs of Dark chaos sands of possibility. Soul is of same "stuff" as upper and lower bowls but frequency band of haphazard interaction is necessarily "tuned" and focused at limited narrows of being. This may be where rationality offers reflection of self in passing through/between energy membrane (glass) with narrows forcing explicit and specific experience. Stuff in lower bowl is of course enriched by scheme of allowing even a very brief aesthetic identity.

With focus and attention, soul power (prayer) may just be glimpsed, (perhaps peripherally) and "true" heart's desire,..... may become evident.

Fighting against fit of work harness may be enough distraction to miss a blink of soul sincerity. Flowing into or enjoying a blanket of attention, integrity and grace may forward a different "type" of resource.

"Stuff" in lower bowl is now enhanced and "flow" has ended. Perpetuity principle flips the hour glass over (not literally) and a somewhat enriched "stuff" flows through a different, perhaps even alien narrows, or one that is similar, thereby being affected by alien, or similar but not of same beauty.

Perpetuity principle is endless and an ever changing "quality" of vital chaos stuff is direction at beautitude.

One might again ask,...to what purpose? This answer is absolutely complete,..... "in order to enhance beautitude with direction."

"As above, so below.".....Hermes. As suggested by Thomas Moore, "there may be a physical presence of soul," and perhaps it cannot be involved by rationality but by a "gravity of sincerity, choice and attention."

This privilege of choice, that citizen has obtained and karmic imagination of experience must weigh in with fractal Dark soul. It is monitor and as having never been apart of complete soul well of chaos possibility,......... is the actual below of Hermes' above.

If "quality" of chaos possibility is direction and purpose at beautitude, soul will need to be attended to with thoughtful and responsible manner. As fractal extrapolation of Dark chaos sea, soul may also be able to extend to unlimited contributors of whatever design.

Experience of identity may lead toward sayings such as "tormented soul," "serene soul" or "soul in love" but each are in fact not really soul-heavy.

Love may be a laying open of soul. When unveiled there would be no inclusion of light. Calamity of spectrum is removed and purpose, possibility and available potentiality are revealed. These may be displayed in emotional form as grace, care, affection and compassion and of course a soul in love is involved in "worship."

Personal involvement with "creation scheme" may suggest why a rational organic in "love" will usually introduce romance, passion and sexual activity. Producing offspring is a purposeful possibility and an available potentiality. It is a simple significant contribution toward enhancement of beautitude with direction.

Has God created rational being in order to worship and enhance God?

A tormented soul might involve an ill-fitting harness or yoke in influencing direction of work moment. With a situation of limited direct pleasing/positive guidance responsibility of choice may weigh heavily and action of experience will be monitored. Actually,... Dark soul will not be tormented as all aesthetics are contributory, but the "fit" with identity may involve war, destruction, fear, misfortune or failure. All are valid, as Dark chaos sea does not differentiate good from evil,.... but identity probably would and that would create hardship in a social, cultural or "civilized" reckoning.

A "serene" soul is without worry or stress. It is calm. Serenity may be a result of ignorance or wisdom. Soul as part of Dark chaos sea of possibility may be a violently textured maelstrom of roiling energy, so once again the phrase is attributed while it is identity and rationality that is described.

Tendency will at first always be to look for soul from rationality but it is from soul that soul must be approached.

Soul has nothing to do with light energy spectrum. It can never be a shining display of vitality. Dark matter as a kind of salt is dissolved in Dark energy. Its active crystalline principle becomes integral in gravity-wave rent. Rationality may be envisioned as a kind of salt distilled from Dark soul energy whose active principle (repetitive internal structure) is maintained at work moment. (offering form and identity)

Although it seems to be a long uphill climb of evolution to rational organic,…. after worship and contribution are over, it is apparently,…. quite an abrupt conclusion. Yet immortality is assured in energy donation,…used and re-used "ad infinitum" though without identity.

Searching in rationality for abnormality of Dark, in even irregular spectrum, light or focus is futile because it is soul, unmanifest even as distortion of phenomena,….but….Dark smells like a salty ocean of creation. Though journey was/is long rationality arrived from Dark.

Salt can be separated from a phenomenal sea by addition of energy. (solar) Dark matter (salt) can be separated from Dark energy sea by addition of energy. (contribution by worshipers) Rationality can be separated from Dark chaos sea of possibility by addition of energy. (nuclear furnace at point creation) These are a few of the unlimited concepts dissolved "with access" in Dark chaos. Even an entire phenomenal light spectrum of a universe is dissolved "with access."

Although it is usually stated that soul is within rationality, a citizen might consider the opposite,…that rationality is within Dark soul. It may be similar to the proverbial "ice cube in water." Created from same essential (chaos) to return to that elemental, but for a "time" an island in a sea of its birth, contributing energy that first influenced separation plus embellishing an essential.

An act of knowing form and identity in situation of "having happened" (aesthetics) giving direction to beautitude and therefore creating "purpose." That being defined as "reason for existence" or "for which creations have been initiated and completed."

Tapping into soul may mean bringing all available heart, emotion, (happy and sad) intelligence, spirit, joy or hate, imagination, inspiration focus and attention from Dark chaos of possibility and into limited cube island realm of manifestation, identity and being.

Key of soul affirms term,…"with access." By definition it allows access. So soul permits access to Dark chaos energy realm of available possibility via itself as having never been apart from said realm and harbors rationality as "visible" distillation of aesthetic.

Aesthetic may spin recklessly around access, yet it is position of the Fifth that might at rim of a galaxian meridian suggest permission to tumble over such an edge of fractal extrapolation of approachable soul into access and illustrate "choice" of identity experience,....to attend,.... and create that experience. (tumblers rotate with "vision" of key) (all disciples did, but Bonesy and the Poet were most notorious)

Aesthetic, (rationality, carbon, silicon or other organic awareness) arriving with soul and directly embellishing Dark realm is significant player, "en masse" in perpetuity principle. Again, it seems to be "fodder," necessary but expendable ingredient that makes scheme "work" as it soaks into chaos sea from plural ones.

This fodder may be an acute enrichment or of a fallow nature.

Citizen of the Fifth will be "paying in attention" and that will result in the "paying" back of energy loan with enriched vitality of experience.

That will contribute to direction of beautitude and that will offer a qualitatively enhanced resource within chaos reservoir. (reason and purpose accomplished) That will begin any subsequent creation with augmented raw essential and that will ensure a next necessary but expendable ingredient. Making such a scheme "work" will be of the acute enrichment type.

When fodder (rationality) is of a fallow nature it is left unseeded and inactive in contribution at beautitude. That may be the way of contemporary rational organic. (citizen of the Fourth) It must donate a maintenance energy parameter but enrichment and embellishment of Dark chaos energy sea will probably not occur.

The situation of achievement as outlined is not presented and "purpose" is not fulfilled in rationality.

This would be a rather tragic situation for any one of the ones. Plural ones will be contributing and enhancement at beautitude is direction and that is still purpose. In perpetuity, Holy trinity continues.

Rationality with identity is however a single experiential occurrence and when over, "stuff" in bottom bowl will be the same as "stuff" in upper. There was no enrichment via identity of experience,...no true aesthetic. A cosmic sadness may be implied by missed opportunity. (live and create freely within light) Positive or negative, opportunity of action within work moment must be embraced in any of an extreme multitude of disciplines across a universe.

Global contemporary rational organic has developed an uncanny ability to produce and participate in all manner of meaningless entertainment. There is significant social reward and notoriety, (at a local level) and even envy in such useless practices that,… do contribute,… but at level of maintaining the minimum monthly payment on an energy loan of experience.

A true creative genius of talent with creative juices flowing through arts, sports, ideologies, sciences and spiritualities will be a major contributor of, shall we say achievement energies. Yet some of the memorable creative musics and mystics have been interpreted as "evil." So be it,…..one way or another it was/is aesthetic and that is the important part.

It is the billions of "hangers on" that need to follow their own creative path.

There is significant group, most of contemporary rational organic, that participates via voyeurism, …..distress, scandal and fortune are fodder of that rationality and it is spread throughout all global societies and cultures at an astounding rate. (basically instantaneous) In many a case validity of this useless social gossip may be untrue or fabricated in order to glamorize it.

Ability to produce and participate in that shallowness is available to anyone with a laptop or phone and production of television programming, videos and short clips (u-tube) is almost completely dedicated to meaningless entertainment.

If harbor of rationality has diminished contribution and possibility wave is beginning to crash over it without finding a refuge for "work and trade," it is a sorry situation.

If potentiality cannot be collapsed that is unreachable but if it collapses and no creative aesthetic can be developed, that is a malfunction of "reason for rationality."

This aesthetic with no further contribution may simply not occur or develop into an unrecognizable situation. Though building of civilizations is a confident rewarding, challenging demand for creative energies the supposed apex of civilizations may suddenly be quite fragile.

Could it change the "position" of rationality in perpetuity principle? Certainly and explicitly for any "one of the ones,"….yes, but do to a variety and diversity of uncountable ones, where-ever and when-ever, contribution and enhanced beautitude as direction,…. will continue to declare "purpose."

Can it be that a fallow field of opportunity may be a necessity? (therefore "purpose" of participants) Is a completion of Four civilizations a "time" to pause and rest advancing great embellishment? (introduction of personal media devices,…such a subtle method) (technological advances arrive only as they are needed) May this contemporary rationality need to contribute via recovery, a fecund state or position in energies of perpetuity principle?

Moving toward the Fifth will need the most fertile fields of possibility, because citizen will use every available soul access to enrich identity aesthetic far, far beyond minimum monthly payment.

Phenomenal tumblers rotating and spinning around key would be focused and in full attention of "vision" of soul. Rationality as aesthetic distillate of chaos possibility could be in full creation mode.

If every rational soul known in identity had a passion of the Fifth that unity may allow extension into unlimited forms, frequencies and methods of contributors. Until the Fifth, rationality as one of ones has been unable to "know" any "other" ones.

However,… rationality has been able to know some of the members of the Fifth that have had their place in time line. Characters of Carpadia were described as first citizens of the Fifth but some might say that they were only first at introduction of the Fifth.

Citizens of the Fifth Civilization of Humankind can be found living in even antiquity of the First. Their contributions have been great and may still be recognized by a contemporary modern, at "darwish" or "sill" of a pending global Fifth.

Pythagoras of Samos, a mystic of Eastern and Western tradition of the ancient world, was thinker, dreamer, pervader of Dark energy of possibility, healer, guru and witness. He was mystic yogi and shaman in respect to a personal non-localized manifestation and associated with seemingly divine attributes and methods of manipulating natural phenomena.

Some of this "magic" may have been learned from an extensive education in Egypt, with supposed tutors from Persia, India, Phoenicia and Chaldean and Jewish mystics.

Pythagoras was a firm believer in "Kairos," "timing" of action, stating that "right moment" was of ultimate importance.

He devised aids that a practitioner might take advantage of in offering a kind of "patience" as a horizon slowly rolled toward and over each pupil.

- a gentleness and contemplation of mind.
- with mathematics and numbers a superior manifestation
- the realm of idea-image that allows soul-vision
- spiritually "alone with the alone" (Ibn¢ Arabi?)
- between phenomenal and incorporeal,....soul key.

Pythagoras designated Monad as a great principle unit and from that Dyad, a foundation of complexity. It was a more basic doctrine than hadras of Ibn¢ Arabi and was a different way of describing same things.

First hadra.....Essence, monad, mystery.
Second and third....Soul of all life.
Fourth hadra...Plato put number into this realm of idea image but Pythagoras originally did not.
Fifth hadra......First manifestation was number and from that "point" and geometry.

In fact, "natural philosophy" of this "magician genius" educated in Egypt, combined astronomy, geometry, music and arithmetic. In attaining utmost command of these subjects, he was able to keep them vital and flexible with each other and eventually with all other disciplines.

Pythagoras systemized his doctrine of numbers and forwarded it into mathematics, and that, into a science conclusive by inference of general principle.

This was absolutely astonishing for a citizen of the Fifth living 500 years before the Christ figure.

Philosophy of this visualization was to put forward ability to focus soul-vision and key and to allow access of Dark chaos sea of possibility. It led to re-designation of number into realm of Fourth hadra of idea image, and promoted "point" to first manifestation.

Contribution of this ancient sage was large into "unveiling" that began to describe phenomenal complexities.

His harmony of spheres and intervals of music inserted his blessed numerology seamlessly into "divine" gift of song and physics of cosmic symbiosis. To say the least such ideas were an imaginative stretching of awareness far, far beyond simply paying time.

Empedocles: "this sage has a unique power of insight capable of seeing beyond spectrum of time and space." His charisma is of special abilities different from an average lay-person. It follows from "attention," focus and deep soul-searching. Though each and every pilgrim would have been given potentiality to transcend the mundane very few have.

Pythagoras, prominent name of Homeric path had an ability to see clearly and intuitively into nature of a complexity. He brought his arithmology into divine properties and then into cosmology. Each number was elemental but "numero uno" was insight, nous, essence and constant, equally respectful and everywhere.

One of the ones was ancient even in antiquity as "order" of contribution. According to Aristotle in "Metaphysics" on Pythagorean doctrine;....."the unlimited and number one for themselves were substance of things of which they were/are predicated. (an extremely ancient description of binary code)

79

There was a Pythagorean renaissance one thousand years after his presence. It occurred in forwarding of a positive view of Kabbala and was basically Jewish mysticism, Neoplatonic-Gnostic tradition with Pythagorean philosophy and Christian theology.

Of course, similarities of gematria and Samos numerology were immediately evident and secret letter associations were, from commonality to the God name that can never be spoken, a duality assumption and marker on "high road" of ability of "mind" to de-couple and lean into soul-key and toward apotheosis.

Pythagoras of Samos, a petitioner of higher glory and keeper of,…. to some extent secret method,…..was magician and genius and citizen of the Fifth living at a time of the First. He was deep into accessing Dark realm of chaos possibility with innocence of extraordinary imagination and attaining and forwarding utmost command of subject and vital flexibility.

Outline of Pythagorean membership of the Fifth adapted from "Pythagoras," Christophe Riedweg, Cornell University, 2005.

One might also suggest that Jesus was a citizen of the Fifth. There are of course so many stories of Jesus of Notzerah. (the man)

It was a time when "Jeshua" was in Tyre. A woman came to him with her daughter bound in rags and tied by waist to her own waist. The child of no more than ten years was filthy with streaks of dried blood across her face and arms, from self-inflicted scratches and bites. The girl was ranting and mumbling.

With a basin of water and cloth Jeshua began to dab at her grime. This was his intense tie with Dark. He was able to reach into chaos that presented as a wretched animal and make it human,….and rational,….. again. He was paying attention, open and looking deep into any possibility. The most simple always endure,….. and what he found was an innocent. Carefully wiping of face and hair brought awareness and with that came appetite. She was fed and grew placid, only just whispering truths that she alone knew.

Jeshua, junior prophet offered herbs to sooth and truth that only the girl knew. He was paying attention. Her mother asked if it was a demon.

His reply,..... "the girl is pregnant, when you find who is responsible you will have your demon,.... you have a young daughter to look out for."

Jesus at this very early time was recognizing his Dark soul and knew that he would have to live the full extent of an extraordinary life experience just to believe it. (it was historically a rational experience and spiritually a contribution of great significance.) It is so when rationality that is aesthetic distillate recognizes aesthetic contribution of enhancement in process of identity. He attended to that by never losing focus of his few disciplines and by never losing their relationships with all other disciplines.

Part of his spiritual ability to manipulate chaos possibility was absorbed in a most learned city of that civilization,....Alexandria. Jeshua jokingly called himself Greek and spoke in several languages. Though probably only a teen opportunities of secular and political banter, of praying the ancient theologies and in confrontation of secret idolatries of Egyptian, Canaanite and perhaps other Semitic peoples offered this young man a very rare and intense environment of query. A simple nomad wanderer came after that time and after an internship with the prophet Yohanan (John the Baptist) who preached to make a way clear for God, Jeshua was able to extend to extraordinary, far reaching "settling points" of imagination. Those being his one true God and Kingdom.

Another simple forgotten "healing." The man was always focused and aware, listening, watching and hearing. At Kefar Nahum on the Demascus road, there was a boy crying in pain with a shin bone jutting out through his skin. He who would be Jesus massaged bone into place and bound it. With a stout splint, the boy walked away. A "miracle" may have been learned in Alexandria in a concentration within which he had become engulfed,...... as a possession. A citizen of the Fifth knows totality of involvement and devotion that was/is. When phrases include responsibility of soul, some understanding of Jeshua may be unveiled. The citizen "owns" that responsibility.

In many ways method in which Joshua "worked" was one of emotional intelligence. It was a sense of rational aesthetic recognized in "being." Experience of it would bring understanding and was his contribution as worship. Jeshua located this realization within himself and in a "kingdom of God." Followers and friends of the time thought this realm might be a kind of dream in which he lived.

So it is with any citizen of the Fifth. The imaginative world is accessed through a Dark soul, sheltered from daily glare of ambition, wealth and ego. In that simplicity of chaos possibility is every faction of becoming, and the Jeshuas need only seek and they will find.

Two quotes:

From the Lord's Prayer;. "for thine is Kingdom, power and Glory, forever and ever."
From Beautitudes;.........."beyond awe, worth and excellence, absolutely
complete in function without beginning or end."

In the Jeshua story and as a citizen of the Fifth, we have a multitude of miracles. What about regularity with which he visited, supped and drank with (from the same spoon and ladle)....... lepers.

Understanding his relations with leper colonies may require understanding lepers and indeed Jeshua understood lepers. He knew that they were shamed by their disease and even concerned that others remain pure. They knew the necessity of a separate "colony" and realized their physical deformities.

Jeshua was shunned at first because of these reasons but when he continued, the lepers as completely rational soul wielding organics,.... let him in. Under this circumstance he could then actually separate diseased members from the group with boils or rashes or any other such afflictions who were sent to the colony prematurely. Of course, these he treated for their minor ailment and sent back to society. From a perspective of commoners these were "cured" lepers.

Jeshua was looking at the human and hardly human in appearance and sorting that out, not isolating those inflicted, and in fact bringing a sense of betterment to a general populace within and outside of colony simply in such keen observations. Lepers, ...being emotional, caring, extremely stigmatized and natural, but for rotting flesh and gnarled bones, and understanding societies fear of impurity (at the time) began to blanket him with normality.

It did not go unnoticed by he who would be Jesus. A depth and amazement to which he inspired was usually not much more then in casual conversation about events outside of colony. Some not hearing of such things for months or even years.

Though they did not realize its significance, he was deeply aware of a difference between outward appearance and inward, of Dark chaos possibility and access via Dark soul. This was a significant theme in all of his teaching. Jeshua could not talk to lay-people of chaos possibility and access so his message was always forwarded via parable and perhaps allegory. (later Jesus would tell his disciples that he had one language for themselves and another for the multitudes)

Possibilities of these smelly disgusting creatures (lepers) though in hopeless affliction,....... contained a humble and timid by isolation,.... voice of normality. So it was in that element of conversation that Jeshua focused, for with eyes closed any voices around the circle were those of an average villager.

Jeshua was always paying "attention" even to smallest details of voice, look or manner. He attended to that with all men and women,... leper, villager, merchant, guard, tax-collector, nobleman and prefect.

In smallest familiarity with idea of Dark chaos sea of possibility is rough and basic rationality of experience brought forth via access of Dark soul in tuning that opportune receiver to frequency of abundance.

With any citizen, as with Jeshua it will sustain, instill or transform a humble vision into a great enhancement and direction of beautitude.

Within citizen (names of the Homeric Path) and within the Fifth civilization is a quintessence, pure extract or essence, the Fifth element. It is that of which rationality, heavenly realms and those far beyond heaven are made. It is Dark chaos storm of all possibility in which even light spectrum is contained.

Jeshua of the Fifth said that the Kingdom of God is like a wind,... in heaven, on earth, within each believer, in-between and beyond. It belongs to no one and to everyone and is every-where and every-when.

He was really saying that Dark maelstrom of energy from which all creations occur is effected by aesthetic contribution, of perhaps rational organic and others, and Dark salt is retrieved from that solution by that energy embellishment. (worship) This Dark matter triggers (is active) possibly like a wind, and gravity rent from "attractions" create point. It matures along a particular line of universal evolution until a servitude is possible. Without identity, it is soul and with identity is rationality.

Reference to wind may have been suggesting active or participatory action within realm and that of a small extrapolation that a believer may claim as property.

An equity of enhancement owned by identity.

That is a true Kingdom, …and a true King of such a realm as was Jeshua who would be Jesus, shall try to guide into this belief. Ability, influence and strength of one knowing this as truth is empowering, and in a time line of opportunity a cusp of the Fifth may only elaborate on the Jesus story. But it was designed for those barely rational,…….. who lived two thousand years ago and it has had many cuts, edits omissions and deletions as it grew into spirituality.

In a more exposed and unveiled situation such ideas as Dark maelstrom, salt, matter and energy pressure nodes may be spoken of more openly. A contemporary psyche in search of soul or purpose is significantly,…. "more rational," though parable and allegoric story are still useful introductory tools. (is there such a situation as more rational?)

It was said that when Jeshua came down from his retreat on Mount Hermon, that the few disciples that he had with him spoke of him there engulfed in a white light of the Lord. Others who had not gone up, particularity Miryam of Migdal saw those occurrences in a different light.

(perhaps via the soul key she possessed into chaos) Miryam said that such a brightness of Lord might be within Darkness of a fundamental with which a creation smithy "worked," ….. in/from,….. his searing crucible. (a rather odd statement that she could not really explain)

Adapted from; "Dark Night of the Soul" by Thomas Moore.

"The Dark within may be crucible of a smithy's forge. Experience of being is pressed upon soul. Anvil is altar of identity where spiritual alchemy manipulates quintessential of possibility into manifestation.

Miryam may have been accurate in suggesting from where a light of the Lord arrived without truly understanding,…. yet "knowing."

Another significant Miryam of the Jesus story is of course his mother, …not Virgin Mary but the biological one. She and her son had quite a difficult time surrendering to each other. Their family underwent two significant moves as brothers and sisters were added on. There was a move from Jerusalem to Alexandria and back to Gallilea. Jeshua and Miryam though constrained by Jewish law and culture in their homeland both grew, learned and flourished in Egypt. (still Jews but in a multi-cultural mecca)

The mother of Jeshua had a phrase that she used when they were in Alexandria,…. "it was as if we shared some kind of Darkness, like people in a shadow corner of place when others went about their business in light."

Miryam was not talking about economics or social station because they became known and respected (in very different circles) in that foreign land. She was talking about the "weight" of a presence that was and was not her own. (possession?) Perhaps they shared a Dark access.

They had Dark souls that did not, in such a magikal place, have an ability to describe usual "settling points." It was so with many peoples and seekers of truth in a city of great libraries and wisdom and yet the most corrupt and vulgar eccentricities describable in that known world.

Many young and old, sages and prophets, thieves and fraudsters loved Alexandria because their Dark souls had found companionship and a "belonging" in that midst. Somewhat sheltered from a glare of dogma, cultural and perhaps moral law, intricacies of accessing Dark sea of possibility and manifesting ideas and realities from a rich fodder of abundance may and did take Jeshua to a greater understanding far beyond even narrow minded elders, scholars and priests of the light.

It was all tolerated and even recognized in Alexandria with so many other eccentricities. As a street urchin of the Dark he began to achieve and contribute in such a unique way. Had he stayed, possibilities of that contribution would have been extraordinary be that socially positive or negative. In such a place, rules of a society were lenient. Yet during certain uprisings in that cosmopolitan energy he was reminded that he was a Jew. He "chose" to accompany his family (that he barely knew) back to the promised land of Jews, so that he might better understand "his" people.

As it would be, the life of Jesus had better than usual energy contribution and the story of it created a,….. "Son of God."

After returning to the "promised" land Jesus preached about his Kingdom of God. Simple listeners and followers thought that it might be just around the corner, or perhaps hidden right before their eyes. He himself seemed to be living in his own special kingdom. (of the Fifth)

That realm was within chaos storm of possibility, with full access via "soul." It was/is just around a corner and barely hidden right before one's eyes. Yet perhaps even the Kingdom of which he spoke was a settling point.

A most un-settling part of it being the inability to "push" beyond heaven………. "Beautitude" will be the covenant of Dark discloser.

(All ideas relating the Jesus story were adapted from; "Testament" by Nino Ricci, Doubleday Canada, 2002)

Citizenry of the Fifth is not bounded by time, though there is approaching,…. a Fifth Civilization. It is a situation when, seeking consciously or not, a greater population of rational organics will realize contribution and therefore begin to comprehend "reason." With that gate open, creative possibilities will flow forth in great abundance.

Richard Feynman was a physicist and great example of a citizen of the Fifth.

He had an ability to "pay attention" concentrate and focus with an energy of application that was so intense that it seemed to arrive from and reside in a different than common realm. (dream-kingdom of Joshua?)

He was also all about understanding things in his own way,… sometime using self-created language and symbols. When his results in physics differed radically from "conventional" wisdom of the time, he would simply go about creating his own wisdom. These are of the most significant permissive qualities of Dark soul of rational being.

There was never such a thing as "settling point" and questions or problems were exhaustively investigated from every conceivable possibility.

Students later said that he continually stressed creativity. In a classroom when a common problem was posited, Feynman wanted each student to arrive at their own solution from their own Dark reservoir of possibilities. It was a concept of personal responsibility.

From Richard Feynman's Nobel prize address:

"Perhaps a thing is simple if you can describe it several different ways without immediately knowing that you are describing the same thing."

It will be simple things that endure, occasionally in unexpected situations. Apart from the truism of unified science an application of psychological and rationally unique directives of persons, fraternities or cultures may have been responsible for diversity of descriptions of Divinity.

Feynman, a scientist was not interested in religion. Perhaps as a citizen of the Fifth even before or during High school, he had already left that far behind.

He would seek into the "unanswered" realm and be granted significant "finding."

With J.A.Wheeler at Princeton an intellectual give and take with Fenman placed them both squarely within citizenry of the Fifth, attaining utmost command of subject and keeping subject vital and flexible. It was in a mutual "faith" that they maintained that simple would endure.

As physicists the two entered into hypothesis and calculation but as great dreamers, wrapped in a cozy blanket of Dark possibility, (as yet unseen) they held perspective of imaginative children (as that is what they were in encountering a quantum neighborhood) and they were able to suspend dis-belief in their "crazy" ideas. (they proposed what became a mainstay of Quantum mechanics by suggesting a virtual particle that utilized negative time value)

It all would require a new way/type of thinking such that freedom within light did not entertain any "settling points."

Feynman went into Dark chaos storm of possibility (perhaps with a pocket full of Dark salt) to demonstrate his ability to manifest a Quantum hypothesis across knowable spectrum all the way from mundane to esoteric.

Yet in all of his very serious work was an obvious quality of "play." He who would play within new-found energies of possibility will be granted an extraordinary finding of "contribution" in embellishment of "beatitudes."

One does not need to return to imagination of children if one has never left it. Children of all of his peers in the world of physics loved his childlike excitement, and he actually entertained them with qualities and properties of physics. It was all fun but when he flipped the coin his "type" of thinking was beginning to illustrate dramatic intensity.

"Is a rational organic necessary to collapse a probability wave function into occurrence?" Complex answer....No

Simple answer......Yes

Richard Feynman was a citizen of the Fifth,...self-taught computational skills and mathematical wizardry, deep intuition of Dark soul, disregard for authoritative contemporary and attainment and vital flexibility of subject. Shweber, a conspirator and colleague from Los Alamos stated that Feynman had "an obsessive need to undo what was secret."

It was said that he encouraged a Feynman mythology, much the way that followers of Jeshua maintained that he,...lived in his own dream.

A hero/heroin who enters Dark labyrinth in order to seek out hidden secrets and treasure would do well to leave a verse-song or yarn along the way. If it should bring them back to a common, (with that philosopher's stone,) they might impart what they could upon an innocent audience.

As Feynman moved slowly into media recognition his popularity with those scientific and lay audiences was secured by a shared Nobel prize in 1965. Then the playful genius with excitement, charisma, and no-nonsense brought a great gift of "wisdom" home to students that would accept it according to each one's capacity.

In intellectual honesty and emotional intelligence, a citizen of the Fifth is focused and involved in contributing "direction" to "beautitude." Due to an enhanced reservoir of Dark chaos sea all other creation will be a "better place."

Feynman looked to seek out a road least trodden. Secret treasures were there to be found. He helped to focus a direction of contemporary physics of the era, but mostly kind of from the sideline. (subtle heroism of citizen)

His later fascination with gravity was deep into an unexplored realm and his intuition was again spot on. In beginning formal discussion of quantum gravitational effects his statement was basically, "not to inquire after a gravitational track, but that which had left it." (hmm,…. KiiJay?)

A citizen of the Fifth must be fearless and confident with their ability to take imagination far, far beyond Harry Potter. In a not so visible realm of physics and computing, Richard Feynman, brilliant soul adventurer, had obtained utmost aesthetic contribution and greatly enhanced and therefore influenced the direction at "beautitude."

This was his and in fact is "the" reason for living as rational organic.

(All ideas relating the Feynman story were adapted from; "Quantum Man" by Lawrence Krauss, Norton, N.Y. 2011)

Staying in a world of physics, shall Albert Einstein be included as a citizen of the Fifth? Probability of such an involvement would suggest,….. yes. There were his famous equations and brilliant intuition as well as an entire life dedicated to physics. In all of that fantastic aesthetic contribution was an actual description of perpetuity principle. Einstein was large in embellishment of direction as purpose at beautitude.

His theory of "general relativity" implies that matter and energy affect the very nature of space itself, allowing it to curve, expand and contract,

(aesthetics) and that this embellished configuration of space (Dark) then affects a subsequent evolution of matter and energy (at point creation) which matures/evolves to a contributory "situation" then continues to impact on space, and so on. (adapted From "Quantum Man.")

Sounds like: Situation of occurrence (matter and energy) as aesthetic of rational organic contributes to Dark chaos energy void allowing expansion, contraction and perhaps a curving or roiling as precincts of familiar donation are manipulated. With Dark chaos sea in an "enhanced" configuration subsequent creation from gravity rent at point (big bang) may mature/evolve into "realization" of contribution and hence embellish via matter and energy, and so on. (perpetuity principle)

"Perhaps an idea is simple and enduring if you can describe it in different ways without immediately knowing that you are describing the same idea."

Two equally intense descriptions of "general relativity" and "perpetuity principle" are gracefully elegant, rough and basic descriptions of a same fundamental triage. Accordingly, sincere dedication of each suggests that vital yet flexible subject will be able to recognize ties with other extreme disciplines.

Physics and religion as aesthetic of rational organic are two of very large fields of recognizable and describable involvement. Almost all inhabitants of this world-place and time would entertain some degree of God influence and it would be a very, very remote assembly of souls that did not make use of contraptions, electronics or motor means, all of which owe manifestation to an unveiling of principles of phenomenal laws.

Adapted from Richard Feynman: "The only reason that this intricate simplicity cannot be unveiled is that there is not yet enough imagination to do so." It may be that an only way to proceed is to "guess" at "quality."

Probability of an unveiling may depend on "value" of such unobservable quality. If those who seek an un-trodden path will have their own, perhaps great treasures will be shared.

"Genius of Imagination" William Duff,... "enlightened, penetrating and capacious mind, rambling and volatile power, perpetually attempting to soar."

Hadras or presences of Ibn¢ Arabi;

First,.....theophany of essence, absolute mystery.
Second and Third,.....angelic, genius, jinn, soul.
Fourth,...idea images of immaterially subtle.
Fifth,.....manifestation of phenomenal.

Imagination presents a creation of its own,....dark essence, access, visualization and finally that which never existed before.

It has driven four civilizations of "unveiling" but unfortunately only within names of "Homeric" path. A good plan might be that within the Fifth fleeting accident prone inspirational genius of a few will become that of many.

Let phenomenal tumblers spin but with attention and soul-key access, bring and support "method" of genius from Dark reservoir.

A kind of "name" must be realized by the hero/heroin "dreamer" of vital subject. It arrives from super subtle hadras of Dark storm accessed by soul-key. Then intense focus and attention of emotionally intelligent rationality to an idea image that is still incorporeal. Finally, a "phenomenal" is unveiled that may present an opportunity for worship and thereby contribution.

Embellishment may be visualized as "mind" hovering over situation as a field/aura of presence, involvement and worth. (rationality)

Mark Kac, international sleuth of magicians and genius, "even after one finally understand what they have accomplished, the process by which they have done it is completely Dark."

Science asks for published transferable "method" and magicians learn and earn their methods but keep them secret. Will a citizen of the Fifth be magician or scientist? One system involves at least recognition by peers and the other only recognition of mystery. Yet the first also now realizes significant recognition of second.

With a personal storehouse of visionary unwritten knowledge citizen may become wizard. Subtly massaging natural laws to suggest the un-natural may be a scientist's Dark discloser. Smell of chaos sea of possibility reeks of magical Dark salt as contemporary science wallows in something quite ancient and simple.

A "dreamer" may hasten, or in a childlike manner span epochs of tedium in fore-fronting truth-set. It was said that Richard Feynman's work was too spontaneously original to observe. Where was he going? In what personal realm was he visualizing? (Joshua) Yet a next step would somehow arrive, perhaps from Divine revelation. (he himself said that he had seen a "name," formulated an idea image and then brought a concept into realization)

He was also aware of a significant limitation,…it was like imagination in a straightjacket due to tight restraints of laws of physics. Work of his science was not freedom of fiction but harness of understanding non-fiction of material phenomena.

Genius of imagination of either and all will write history of rational organic in spectrum of "being" and of "having happened."

That,…one might recognize as embellishment, is contribution to Dark chaos sea of possibility and in so gives direction at beautitude gate and hence is "reason" for doing so.

Though science tends to unveil as needs arise simplicity of understanding "purpose" will hopefully un-wrinkle a few brows and allow imagination a less hindered quest for unveiling.

The "what if" scenario is not for a true citizen of the Fifth.

Realm of mind, floating above neurological substrate, looking upon self, is of Dark soul heavy access in rationality. (not usually associated)

Vitally flexible energetic atoms are everywhere on near side of a cross weft, entangled pressure energy membrane. They are reflected by but are not "in" that mirror. Troubling "infinities" of physics will not be undone by quantizing. The phenomenal is only fastidious to a "point."

A Feynman guess at model clarity;…. before a mirror left is right and right is left but up and down are still same. A question arises from an axis running "through" a mirror. There are knowingly only two situations exhibiting action along such an axis, ….big bang and black hole.

Symmetry and asymmetry:
-building towers and cities/ mountains and forest
-pipes and plumbing/ rivers, lakes and streams

-electric current/lightning
-DaVinci man over eclipse/ offset of all animal organs

Suggestion and conservation of "parity" may only be phenomenal up to a level of organic molecule. Only right-handed molecules of sugar beets are digestible by bacteria, why not those that are left handed? Gell-Mann's long weekend of transferring co-ordinates back and forth without proof, suggested conservation of "parity" simply as phenomenal fact. Yet that is not parity "by nature." (soul symmetry/ animal asymmetry)

Within calamity of spectrum, smart atoms in extremely complex arrangement are what one sees in entangled pressure membrane mirror of cosmic background radiation. Reflection is very precise (excluding parity) and possibility of complex identity crossing along a "through" axis is zero.

Natural occurrence is asymmetrical (why are heart organ and others offset?) (why freedom of choice?) and that may be an irritating quality of contribution to a symmetry of homogenous dark chaos with direction. It does not disrupt beautitude because in an absolute "completeness" is allowed purpose and hence "reason for."

Irritant that is rough and basic privilege of choice that citizen has obtained and karmic imagination of such experience must still weigh in and perhaps somehow balance with fractal Dark soul.

"Inherent fuzziness" (uncertainty principle) of phenomenal situation and its irritating qualities are abruptly forwarded from dissident to consonant. An unstable inconsistency that is energetic contribution of rational organic is then embraced by Dark chaos storm, as arriving home, without ambiguity of rational motive.

A relatively long road around for smart atoms of cosmic furnaces, yet instantaneous until rationality. Dislodged and uniquely experiential (by association) Dark energy of possibility is temporarily harnessed to/ with photon, neutron, electron, etc. to support nano-biological evolution toward organic molecule and eventual worship. One of the ones and a situation as ancient and simple as yesterday.

If beautitude was to be slightly incomplete it would be imperfect but/so in its completeness,… with direction,… is perfection.

(lacking nothing essential, having all necessary and familiar characteristics required for a given situation, as in one of the ones, absolute emphasis of category extent)

Must perpetuity principle and access to chaos reservoir of possibility be specialized in order to create? They must be "active" with tools of pressure/buoyancy, Dark matter gravity rent and point creation.

What would be a generalization from which they were differentiated?

Reservoir of "that which will have occurred" can be "named" future perfect medium of Dark. Once unveiled perhaps some ingredients of description will/have slipped through a marriage of hadras and into manifestation.

There is an idea image of request modifier that forwards imagination into irritant of imposition. Perhaps a perturbing theory authored by disruption and a troubling of status quo. That which signals a harbor of commerce?

Order and chaos change polarity at S4 paddle of gravity alpha helice on pressure membrane mirror, initiated by Dark matter coming out of solution. (analogy pending)

As purpose, that will allow gate specialization of Dark storm and perpetuity principle in order to interact with "aesthetic" of flawed smart atom of material spectrum.

Reservoir of future perfect possibility may be a pristine Dark inventory of a truly inconceivable all. Direction requires action and an active loading dock/gate of "beautitude" may be differentiated essence of contributing purpose.

"Beautitude" is: "the continually enhanced gate of chaos cauldron of possibility,….forever enriched by aesthetic donation,…beyond awe, worth and excellence, and in that process absolutely complete in function without beginning or end."

It may be necessary to put one foot after another into a river of potential in order to cross to reservoir. Once one has crossed, in Buddha's favorite example, one can leave supportive tools of enlightenment, (literature, music, physics, philosophy, mathematics, etc.) on the far shore.

"Activity" of beautitude is perfect and future perfect reservoir of "that which will have occurred" has need for aesthetic imperfection by which to measure purpose. In a very, very simple minute "sense," .....enter rationality,...........a familiar rational organic has purpose."

Does it again seem a horrendously long way around? Not so without time and rationality is self-admittedly a position of "uncertainty." In that may be absolute necessity of "confusion of choice" or "option" as aesthetic of rational contribution.

Aesthetic imperfection is "option,"...time limited opportunity.

Probability wave function only "collapses" into manifestation when the decision of an observation is applied. A "fuzzy" aspect of uncertainty principle is an irritant relative to perfect activity of beautitude, as gate of future perfect reservoir of Dark inventory in a truly inconceivable all.

If perfection is fundamental of reservoir, then again, in such a thing as "option" there may be irritant and hence embellishing directive of pearl formation.

There must be a "quality" of purpose, perhaps only peripherally glimpsed by a fractal-extrapolated position within Dark soul.

It is divinity becoming aware of divinity, via the "flawing" of smart atom,...non-local until observed,...and rational dependent.

References from science and physics adapted from "Genius" James Gleick, Vintage, N.Y. 1992

-Inconceivably abundant reservoir of future perfect possibility.
-Beautitude as a gate,...specializing action of differentiation.
-"Method".......genius, imagination and magic.
-Symmetry, asymmetry and parity.

"Order is time limited option of chaos possibility."

Order with rationality and soul as fractal extrapolation of Dark, always maintains simple complexity of disorder. In relationship with house and vehicle they, like all fundamentals (electro-dynamics) will reverse attitude (pendulum conspiracy) in order to present/forward access.

When polarity of organic molecule is involved at voltage gated ion channel a potential difference is introduced across a plasma membrane. Alpha helice is voltage sensing at perhaps nodal interface. Electromagnetic field induces conformational change. In the new "open" state ions begin to flow and that energy transfer or "trigger" manipulation begins a process of doing "work." (as below, so above) (voltage gated ion channel) (Wikipedia)

When energy polarities are involved at cosmic background radiation mirror membrane, a precinct of familiar nodal energy will become critically buoyant. That pressure invites Dark salt out of solution of Dark chaos energy sea and in presenting, Dark matter will incur the trigger of Gravity rent,… alpha helice of Gravity. With induction of conformational change energy flow of familiar possibility escapes into "point creation" and that begins the process of doing "work."

Multitude eons after this event,…. rational organic may occur. If so,.. it will with aesthetic donation forward experiential mayhem back to Dark chaos reservoir of possibility.

"Position" of rational organic may be "one" part of fodder in perpetuity principle, beautitude and abundance. "Fodder" as described by Encarta World Dictionary:…."the expendable ingredient that makes a system "work."

"Method" of genius and magic of imagination is an ability to go to essentiality and to bring bits of it forward, according to capacity of self, within authority and versatility of subject. Without extremely, extreme focus the "random" will cloud and shroud this pure "empty set."

In standard "set theory" of axioms and by existential principle there can only be one set with no elementals. It is the idea image of "beautitude" as access to future perfect reservoir of possibility. ("the" empty set, not "an" empty set)

Dark limitless chaos sea of possibility may magically present as "the" empty set and in a conception of George Cantor's transfinite numbers:…. "an infinite set may be placed in a one-to-one correspondence with "one" of its subsets." (pause) "an infinite set may be placed in a one-to-one correspondence with "one" of its subsets."

"prayer of God, prayer of humankind, dialogue with Divinity"

Poem from "The chronicles of Vanisila"…..Fox
> Feel dryness in rain, hear silence in thunder,
> Touch illusion, live asunder
> Eyes surge Dark power, breath is Arctic fire
> Truth of tongue, eternal liar.
> Present in absence, den of crystal salt
> Bleed a shadow, feed on stagnant wind.
> Mutant moment, rape innocent time,
> No thing lives in nothing.
> Invest myth, imaginative genius,
> Settle not, implore a genus
> One of ones.
> Spectral interval, Dark
> Correlative realms, and……

So how might the inaccessible be accessed,….but by retracing a fractal extrapolation of itself. Vehicle might be available not by crossing essentialities but by apprehending and holding very close to heart a vital, intentional desire to magically display "method."

It would certainly involve soul.

Adapted from "Natural Grace"…. Fox / Sheldrake

Via Positiva,……….	"experience of awe, wonder, gratitude. rendering self vulnerable to awe."
Via Creativa,……….	"honor and pay attention to idea-image, respect a deeper insight."
Via Transformativa,…	"compassion, healing, interdependence, concept of sharing"
Via Negativa,………..	"letting go, nothingness, emptying."

Meditation on a mantra,…...   letting go of words but keeping sound.
Meditation on a soul,…...   letting go of order but keeping chaos.

Pythagoras, Cantor and Feynman are indeed true names of the Homeric path of order in number, yet are there others, …perhaps quasi-numerical?

May even Moses be associated with numerology? He states in the Old Testament that "creation" took six days. Perhaps not because it took place in a period of time, but because bringing it into existence necessitated "order" and order is synonymous with number. This assumes presence of rational organic, not a particularly supra-human being. (Pythagoras,….number as first essential) (gematria of mystic Jews)

(Feynman and Wheeler on virtual participant in negative time)

The most appropriate number for creation was 6. The first perfect equaling both product and sum of essentials 1,2,3. Order began immediately at point creation, even without "rationality" of organic? Creation as sum/product of masculine plus feminine times infinite set, placed in a "one-to-one" correspondence with one of its subsets.

Four, was foundation of ten. (and on the fourth day was an unveiling of heaven and earth) One to four plus,… equal ten,…. turn of order. One is point, two line, three surface and four solid, therefore first corporeal. Four is first square and is consonance and sharing and as such is beginning of realm of "sharing." Sharing is primary characteristic of rationality. So what of ten? (Rosicrucian Library, vol. XLI, Universe of Numbers.)

Is turn of sequence fundamentally based on concept of one of ones in dialogue with infinite, (empty) set? Numerically it "is" a one and a zero.

Are "formal' and "material" geometries of Robert Fludd truly balanced across the board? What number comprehends all substance and quantity and how does it relate to "empty set?" Is contemporary technology based upon this simplicity?

When values of visible and invisible oscillate less widely, (James Hillman) an accessible nudges up against an inaccessible in a relatively extreme display of intent, desire and knowledge.

Socrates considered ignorance a kind of evil, yet it is sometime considered a type of bliss. (proximity may be subjective) A dedication toward some form of enlightenment might be a calling of "rationality" though the disregard of any such directive will still maintain aesthetic contribution to/of chaos energy. (especially with generations of contributors)

How can unity of "chaos realm" of future perfect reservoir create complexity of "order?" With beautitude as gate and perpetuity principle, (holy trinity) a "chaos game" may present.

Numerology of this process includes a "random" and a "simple."

Cosmology of same might include thrice lucky binary turn-style of gravity rent on cosmic background radiation pressure membrane at buoyancy saturated "familiar" nodule.

Result,…random producing order. A method of producing "attractor point" in any "iterated function system." It is a simpler method of drawing fractals from Dark storm toward and into "soul."

In process of extremely large numbers of "ones" cosmic repetition factor would be at least as "thick" as an RNA template for formation of amino acid and DNA life blocks in tireless and perhaps boring struggles in creation of "life."

Such a "chaos game" is not time specific and one will have to remember the old tongue in cheek definition of infinity: "a thousand primates sitting at type writers will eventually produce the entire text of War and Peace."

Rational organic may be included in such an extreme order but supplement of beautitude will also continue from untold numbers of ones. The concept is very large. This principle is so "unfathomably" unique that it must be abundant. Simple things will endure.

"Binary" and "duality" qualities present in everything from religious philosophy to sex and are even now found in far cosmic reaches,….not to mention ALL technology,….. illustrate the simplicity of zero and one.

Simple, common and everywhere, cosmic spectrum and empty set, place-holder column and "unit" will display a "turn of order." From Moses story: "creation did not take place in a period of time, but coming into existence required order and that is synonymous with number."

Turn of sequence may be first visionary suspension of dis-belief in forwarding complexity of "imaginative situation." That goes a long, long way back toward chaos and that "magic" has been "hidden" in a labyrinth of the obvious.

It required Feynman and Wheeler to collaborate and reassure each other's sensibility in suspending disbelief and diligently pursuing an imaginative idea of virtual particles in negative time.

Extension of Dark chaos realm of possibility is held within soul as fractal extrapolation of principle, ...a minute portion that is identical to the impossibly familiar idea image of,...that from which creation occurs.

Many repetitions of numerological calculation may illustrate finite complexity and hence blossoming aesthetic quality. As in a Mandlebrot set, zooming in reveals/unveils familiar, similar, complex pattern. Soul is patterned after chaos and zooming out unveils/reveals Dark library of possibility, holding spectrum and compartmentalized unilateral complex rational organic.

"Situation" may be described as "changing at a changing rate."

(similar to third derivative of foundation of motion) A citizen contributes at an increased rate of imaginative disbelief and hence forwards creativity far beyond a strait jacket of physical manifestation. Chaos theory as aforementioned suggests order from/in chaos. Binary technology may infer fractals as a fractional dimension. Unveiling of which may describe a "familiarity" of/within beautitude. (as "this" gate)

Iteration is an obvious simplicity. Values in a fractal tending toward infinity approach Dark chaos realm and values that tend toward zero approach Dark chaos realm. It might seem that any "one" was surrounded by Dark chaos realm. A contributing simplicity may suggest that of course, in several disciplines,.... this,..... in all probability would not be disputed.

"Point" is "situation" and that is contribution of aesthetic irritant to beautitude and hence future perfect reservoir of possibility. Such a state may tend toward equilibrium but for the requirement of "purpose."

A grand scheme needs (or does not need) a massive vault that does not get involved in any loan/payment energy exchange in respect of necessary momentum-equity. Peripheral interaction of nodal energy, Dark salt, gravity rent and point creation is a relatively small process though involving every phenomenal display everywhere and every-when.

When cosmologists gaze out into a star studded Darkness do they focus upon the multitude perturbations? What if a balance across relic microwave-background-pressure-energy-mirror-membrane required an equal number of "vents" in the opposite direction?

"Fabric" is starting to sound more and more appropriate. Why wouldn't any membrane require a fundamental "breathing" in order to prevent a catastrophic rupture? In perpendicularly woven membrane of a specific pressure energy weft as fabric, will there be intersecting "nodes" of familiar precinct vitality?

Balance at pressure energy fabric may be maintained by billions of souls of rational organics and many billions of other "ones" in their relative phenomenal theaters. Size and temporality in those realities will be comparative only with a familiar "one" that is made aware of "it."

Possessing "soul" as fractal extrapolation of Dark chaos sea of possibility, "alternative" rational being will exist in experience, evolve, worship and contribute via their particular experiential aesthetic, monitored by a great unified soul idea that forms "vents." These "vents" are soul connections with divine force of creation. (future-perfect Dark chaos sea of possibility)

If balance must be maintained a horrendously large system of gravity rent, star point creation toward evolution of rationality and equally grotesque returning mayhem of energy of contribution of choice and imagination,….. may of necessity exist everywhere and every-when.

A fundamental "breathing" is accomplishment of balance. It is harmony and equality of debt and credit, the acceptance of energy loan and "lifetime" of "paying attention." Each extremely unique situation is personal possession and that is ownership and that must be held in the highest regard as dialogue with divinity, or as in realm of trans-finite number:...... "an infinite set may be placed in a one-to-one correspondence with "one" of its subsets." (in a time) (George Cantor)

Occurrence is very unique and personal, guarantees contribution and "involvement" and as such it has a very simple reward and will probably endure. In fact, this principle is so "unfathomably" unique that it must be abundant. A "gift" of contribution of experience (all of its choices and options) is,.... everlasting contribution without choices and options. This is exactly what "happens." (without identity)

Of course, aesthetic of occurrence is simply "valid." In such an almost inconceivably vast imaginative idea, ...there would be no place for relative concepts such as good and evil, here and there, then and now. Those would be specific "within" situation and to a large extent subjective.

This may be allowing imagination out of the phenomenal straight-jacket to describe phenomena in simple terms of energy exchange and contribution. Since $E = mc^2$ everything seems to be in "order."

In mythology of physics, mythology of Haida of the N.W, mythology of number, mythology of the San of Namibia, mythology of Mayan long count, or even Carpathian myth story and mythology of "empty set theory" there will be nodes of familiar precinct vitality as weft of imagination.

From :   "A Story as Sharp as a Knife" (Robert Bringhurst).... "Raven flies through cloud-mirror in the sky to bring back skin of new-born."

From: "Hero with an African Face" (Clyde Ford)...."Atunda is that which ends contribution and yet supplies energy for creation."

From: "Aristotle on Metaphysics" .... "Unfathomable and unit of participation are ideas displayed as predicate calculus."

From: "Genius" (James Gleick)...perhaps from George Cantor,... "an infinite set may be placed in a one-to-one relationship with "one" of its subsets."

From: "Popul Vuh" (Dennis Tedlock, translation).... "revealing would be everything under sky to four corners and to know and acknowledge beyond that to the "long count."

As Feynman said;..."discoveries of true presence and reasonable phenomena have not yet been unveiled due to insufficient imagination."

So any citizen of the Fifth must be willing to suspend disbelief and recognize "beautitude" as not only "gate" of familiar rational organic "situation" of future perfect possibility, but "a" gate at each point creation of "all" situations of future perfect possibility. It is another extremely simple probability.

"Beautitude"......... "the continually enhanced gate of chaos cauldron of possibility,...forever enriched by all forms of aesthetic donation,...

beyond awe, worth and excellence and in that process, absolutely complete in function, without beginning or end.

So if interwoven entanglement of pressure energy fabric as mirror membrane, recognized in the universe of this rational organic as "relic" micro-wave background radiation, is extremely porous in both directions, then their hardly seem to be unbreachable "walls" in vision of "being," that the citizen of the Fifth will "settle" upon and declare limit.

Beautitude is gate,... reservoir of future perfect (that which will have become) is chaos sea of all possibility,... soul is "vent" accessing everything dissolved in that sea,..... and perpetuity principle and holy trinity are creators of universe.

If creators of "one" universe, then creators of all universe. If soul idea is "vent" in familiar rational organic then it is also "vent" in alternative rational organic. These are "tools" of beautitude,...and as above, so below,.... a dock, or gate is necessary ingredient of "action" that maintains commerce. That is direction and that supports purpose.

How does commerce work so well in time line of rational organic? How many generations of rational organic have strived to create/maintain commerce? Probably due to necessary ingredient of this "action" that has been instilled as direction supporting purpose. Perhaps it is much more fundamental than that.

If this is part of quality of being then in case of "just barely out of animal" there will be basic communications of work and reward. Be it for food, clothing, shelter, mobility, support, sharing, family, neighbors, or general altruism and in that as with religion, again reward in the belief in positive afterlife.

Contribution does result in direction supporting purpose (without identity) though a fundamental in rationality may be as simple as commerce, ...work, trade and reward. (actual energy manipulation toward beautitude)

Design of "civilization" has basically been acknowledged as a sharing, emergence of participation in "order" to work, trade and attain reward.

A question/answer may occur in the common belief that each individual, private "vent," (soul connection with the divine energy of creation) does in fact believe that all other separate "situations' (individuals) also have their own "vents."

This is a startling idea. How is that?

With absolutely no proof or even remote possibility of proof it is still quite simply believed. Is it a factor of wanting it to be, ...so that in trust of others being like the "one" known experience they will work to accomplish and therefore be in compliance with "goals" (rewards) of the "one" knowable work moment? ....probably.

So with that in mind and a principle of "alternative rational organic,"....commerce, contribution, and un-provable trust, should put "them" in compliance with goals and rewards of their only true "one" knowable work moment?

In such an idea, all "vents" every-where and every-when are so unfathomably unique that they must be extremely abundant. With that volume of soul access bridging an entangled pressure energy fabric, balancing instances of action of Holy trinity in gravity rent and point creation would be nothing less than a pretty big bang.

Evolving and maturing principles may require a lot of time, but that principle itself does not exist until rationality. Ultimate cosmos may only exist in work moment. (Dasein on its way toward reward)

It is also interesting to note that true presence and reasonable phenomena completely break down and become un-knowable at quantum of extremely small and at massively large. These both being in realm of ability to bridge entangled pressure energy mirror fabric. Is that a caution?

One may not ever maintain rationality and "bridge" fabric.

Soul connection as fractal of future-perfect possibility in hour-glass narrows of Dark chaos sea is the only bridge that can occur in "familiar zone" of rational being.

From Dark storm arrives directive of action and via mayhem of choice and option returns contribution of irritant into eternal homeostasis. Such a system will require a "gate" or "dock" for commerce of purpose and that as,..... "forever enriched by aesthetic donation,.... is beautitude."

"Brick" that is familiar zone of rational being has therefore an intangible mortar holding it in place and contains an internal and integral portal that provides extra strength in holding up the sketchy wall of perception. (soul is in rationality and rationality begets soul)

Perhaps "unit" of such brick is flawed smart atom,......flawed because it must involve observation in "order" to be localized and that must be a characteristic of rationality.

The extreme porous quality of cosmic micro-wave background radiation is "peripherally" in mortar and internally in hollow core of brick rational flawed smart atom. As such, placing of any wall of this type is at best very sketchy and temporary. In scheme of temporality this is large-obvious including an idea that temporality does not exist without rationality.

Internal and structure strengthening hollow would be soul vent with future perfect chaos reservoir and peripheral incorporeal mortar component might be "aura of self" that sustains presence, location relative to other rational organics, unit contribution and identity. This aura of self is gravity of belief. (with limits) It is opinion that there is existence and a reality when there is no absolute proof of existence or reality.

In fact, at quantum of extremely small and ultimately large suggestion is that existence and reality of familiar rational organic has no presence without observation by rational organic and that frequency of occurrence of "one" incidence is so short that it falls into a category of "uncertainty."

So, what is in the belief that all other rational or "alternative rational" organics have soul connection with Dark chaos storm of possibility? Why is it "simply believed,"..... with personal possession of same? Within a principle of uncertainty is there really more than instinct and appetite?

If this awareness and cosmological location are a "system" then there is no causality within any of it. This awareness and cosmological location are a "system." Place holder column and the "one" of this completeness are simple contribution to "purpose." Alternative rational organics are contribution to purpose outside of this "system," and an idea of uncertainty "is" in both/all systems,.... more than instinct and appetite.

Animal may never be uncertain but only balancing options of approach but a rational may truly be uncertain.
Is this again a sample of flawed smart atom?

So, rational organic has continually moved a pawn step forward without angular capture until the Fifth. Have not our first and pre-ancestors.....also been here? Why simply believed? Yes,...hope for a system in concept of familiarity, yet "alien" is by definition,...not familiar.

As such, alternative rational organic cannot ever be "present" in familiar cosmological unity, even out to limit of Star Ship Enterprise.

Perhaps similar to familiar knowable universe are unlimited alien universes that are contributors to beautitude and hence "purpose" in round-about that describes "reason." Any type of action infers growth and that must have purpose.

Assuming that all unlimited alien universes have soul connection with Dark chaos storm of possibility, (which would be probable from inference of the one knowable soul situation) then the magnificent scheme of contribution from every unimaginable direction and temporality may in the Fifth begin to open the other 90%.

When "felt" and "known" and "dreamed" and "amnemnatic" and possibly "intuited" and imagined via the extreme "magic" of an angular capture, become…… "possession." ……it may be an understanding that activates a few billion more synaptic junctions then what were common transit of awareness in the previous Four. In fact the envisioned "map" of a complex multi-dimensional "firing" such as will occur at possession of the Fifth, may look very similar to the greater then cosmological round-about that describes reason and "reason."

If that situation turns out to be more than just similar but same, then a soul-pulpy vented rational organic contributor suspended only within a mortar of peripheral, incorporeal "aura of self" may truly be an active-player-recipient of any and all possibilities of Dark chaos storm. (by design, which suggests "purpose")

Why does gravity of belief sustain? (within limits) If scheme of contribution from every unimaginable direction and temporality lays open, then "creation" is not only as abundant as perceived but virtually and critically far, far into a very serious realm of imagination. Citizen of the Fifth should go there. (Richard Feynman: … physical laws of the phenomenally manifest are not yet describable because we simply do not have enough imagination.)

It could be from this point creation that Dark soul will salt tumultuous Dark energy sea of possibility to "push" that which was dissolved with access within imaginative chaos to bring forth, or unveil a presage of true "passion of the Fifth."

Imagine exotic and mundane, absolutely un-provable realms of existence and reality encountering one another. It may be a bit of a stretch, because alternative rational organic cannot be "present" in familiar cosmological awareness/unity.

Perhaps the idea may require retreating to a "magical" term. Ask about an "omen" hinting at "aprenda" of actual future perfect,… "that which will have been done." Soul "key" in this is "will" and that may be portal conclusive and inclusive in direction of quest oriented stretching of imagination far enough to apprehend "felt, known, dreamed, amnemnatical and possibly intuited angular capture."

When extreme aesthetic art form of such an imagination is created, how would citizen move into it. Do they "push" unveiling with familiar? Is that like including a can opener in every can? A fecund condition of this "type" of virtuoso may be due to access and excess. Portal that strengthens by realizing void at center of brick rational flawed smart atom is "touching" great overabundance with that same hollow soul force that "it" is made from. To paraphrase an ancient poet,..."Foxy licks chaos salt, he assumes quality of interval in spectrum and is able to sniff out a void from heavily veiling scents."

"Scent,"...(Encarta World Dictionary)...a hint left behind that is useful or diversionary when tracking. To detect a faint suggestion of an imminent.

Fractal extrapolation of Dark chaos of all possibility is soul and therefore,..... same as.

"Moving into" is accomplished by getting close and staying very near soul. As rationality continues small steps along path, it will be soul that captures imagination with subtle, alien angle of attack. This passage may be so innocuous that citizen declares,.... ..."where did "that" come from" as they realize the can is opened.

An ever-humble citizen now resides in an extreme aesthetic, supercharged, imaginative art form and is the virtuoso that will perform it flawlessly.

That is nature of the Fifth. These flavorists, understanding isolation and blend, coax a frothy melody from white noise of Dark chaos sea and then suggest harmony, interval and imaginative spiritual intelligence of,.... "familiar leaning into alternative,".... rational situation. It is an "understanding" because an "alternative rational organic" cannot be "present" in familiar cosmological unity. (if and when it is then it has become "familiar")

The furtive grasp may be as Ibn¢ Arabi suggested,..... recurrence of like but not same. This ancient Persian was a member of the Fifth.

108

Isolation and blend,.....“keep self and subject vital and flexible in ties with all other disciplines.” (Herman Hesse.....Glass Bead Game..... citizen of the Fifth)

Perhaps this is relatively basic creativity, considering the imaginative stretch in order to suggest “a virtual particle using negative time value.”

(Feynman and Wheeler ......both citizens of the Fifth)

The dreamer of the Fifth may not only utilize a method of genius but “be” a method of genius. (relative to transit of the previous Four)

“Genius,”.....(Encarta World Dictionary)........ “Special and different quality that is unveiled at a particular location, temporality and basic awareness. As an alien idea understood as a supernatural “demon,” and as in all cases, ...extremely influential.”

So, as each member of citizenry of the Fifth begins to construct intense imagination they will not expand time and space. These are still only and specifically integral with their own cosmos. They will not substitute an exquisite experience of contribution with an alternative option. The continually enhanced gate of chaos cauldron of possibility, forever enriched by aesthetic donation, is beyond awe, worth and excellence, and in that process, absolutely complete in function,....... without beginning or end.

A genius dreamer of the Fifth will unveil guidelines of next and probably final civilization of humankind,....“Passion of the Fifth.”

Demon, evil spirit and Daimon, divine power are equally present in Dasein. Are they any more or less imaginable then “virtual particles in negative time?” These, and “everything” else, even and especially if not corporeal are all qualities of the same thing. (they have to be)

Was there an omen?....an indicator of direction of temporality?...a scent?....faint suggestion of an imminent, ...or a soul pulpy hint of,..... that which will have been done?

It may simply be a gift comprehensible. Alternative rational organic can never be present in “familiar” cosmological awareness/ unity, but that does not mean that it does not exist. Such an encounter may need be an “understanding” of process of involvement between rationality and cosmology to hence suggest that such a process is simple and mundane and must be common. Idea of contribution utilizing perpetuity principle to enhance beautitude and thus impart "purpose" upon Dark chaos sea of possibility is so to the extreme,….. routine,…. that it must be everywhere and every-when and involve everything. (including all alternative rational organics of whatever composition)

Imagine the ignorant arrogance of putting forward an idea that humanity as rational organic is alone and special.

Flawed smart atom of all realities and uncertainty principle must be present in "each" case as function of containment, (and separation) yet all are by design,….. contribution. Only in an imaginative, soul pulpy hint of "that which will have been done" can citizen aspire toward a future perfect realm. (it is location always perfectly positioned in future)

If contribution is energetic abundance with purpose and soul is tendril of connection directly with that chaotic ocean of mayhem then citizen must find and stay very close to that delicate, wispy curl of Darkness that each "one" has as possession, for in understanding of "that" is complete "living freely within light." (that may be a "purpose")

When a complete civilization of humankind attains this awareness then future perfect realm of "thy will have been done" shall be in occurrence.

It may put one, many or even possibly …all?…. at advantage, in order to influence the temporal event. Living freely would suggest,…. without recognizing "fundamental differences between rational organics" and of course "that" whole idea is finally disappearing very quickly. Without mediait would disappear sooner.

It was spoken of in ancient Persian lore. "Creation of extreme imagination exists only within this faculty until by "himma" a true gnostic citizen of the Fifth unveils that which will assume form outside of this faculty." In service of soul,…… creativity fulfils primary aspect of intention/function. (Alone with the Alone, Ibn¢ Arabi))

When comprehending and activating "hadras" of becoming, …..."purpose," ….is overflowing from the great reservoir of chaos possibility and spiraling toward unique cosmologies of any and all rational or alternative rational results of unlimited point creation by Holy trinity.

(rationality is not guaranteed, and many do not achieve)

This theater has a prehensile quality initially and then an iconic value slips in until active participation in work moment may have to be extremely disciplined in "order" of dreaming the "understanding." It is a worth-while endeavor.

Players give and take a turn and all are actors of script in process. A handful of Homeric path and members of citizenry have been capable of a presentation, yet all citizens in possession of Dark soul have the same potential and that is within access and excessive taking of Dark chaos realm of all possibility. Take it in any complex wandering, adventure, striving or studying manner that any "one" can imagine.

There is a time limit. The atom, as smart as it is, still has its inherent flaw. "It must involve observation in order to be localized and that must be a characteristic of rationality." Soul is not that smart. Really, no "one" ever said it was. Basic chatter has usually been about non-rationality of soul. Hundreds or more plays, songs, films, symphonies and poems have expounded upon vulnerabilities of,….. "that which everyone believes everyone else has with absolutely no chance of proof."

(still a very unique idea)

Time limit of flawed brick smart atom is rationality. It is both rational organic unit and unit of rationality. It is at corner of Gersmer and Titeran and in corner stall of Tunisian casbah. It was not in Siberia with pre-mammoths or on lowland dry sea beds of the Dakotas with dinosaurus simplistic.

Those were not even "events" unless brick smart atoms in those configurations were "observed," …. though form of brick smart atom as fossil and feces suggest a significant "proof."

All of cosmology may only be a maintenance level situation. More scrutiny would probably never-ever suggest anything more than that. Billions of failures and perhaps a success,… per each maintenance level situation,…..of billions of opportunities of maintenance level situations will occur in the billions. (the term billions just being a reasonable far reaching speculation, though extent would be limitless)

So,….what of flawed smart atom when not observed?

Michael Markevich

Flawed smart atom as principle characteristic and brick of manifestation, is penetrated by soul and held in containment and separation by mortar of possession.

Adapted from "The Divine Matrix" by Gregg Braden/ Hay House, 2007.

"Familiar rational organic is a control measure of containable separation within which cosmology exists, ...a bridge between measurable and imagination ......and a mirror that reflects creative ambition.

It is an artist's expression of/on quantum fractal canvas and is said,.... fabric and image, paint and brush, atom and observation."

Flawed smart atom when not in interaction of "participation" which it must be, in familiar quion of phenomenal, should probably be "in potentia," ....and eternally imminent.

Participation suggests an act in process. It is unfinished. When contribution by rational organic is complete "Dasein" is no longer available but perpetuity principle will continue to be justly defined as will Dark chaos storm.

As eternally imminent is it a state of future perfect? Is it position perfectly positioned in future? Or is it sometime attainable throw of cosmic dice possibly resulting in an "ideal" situation of contribution?

"In potentia" means,... possible but not yet realized and realization is flaw of participation, irritant that must be covered in layers of time in order to create valuable "pearl." That being localization of flawed brick smart atom.

Applied temporality allows work moment according to capacity and that will be contribution. Time limit for contribution is rationality and within that contained separation smart atom can be localized. It is the "moment" of a single complete cosmology.

A beautiful gift of companionship with an entire cosmos of souls.

(still a very unique idea)

So,.....a citizen might not want to lose sight of "moment." It is possession and like the, still very unique idea, may very well be an "only" opportunity of cosmos and contribution with uniqueness,....

112

yet,…. somehow sharing,….. of identity. (in fact probably commonly routine)

A significant alien rationality may not even understand why familiar rational organic cannot understand "potential." Brushed over and then ignored in favor of manipulating a lingering "alpha-animal" hierarchy situation "in potentia" is extremely limitless relative to position within tribe.

To go forth into perhaps a single creative "hadra" can bring into realization and manifestation a novel situation within compliance of the known, and perhaps "push" physical boundaries. How many patents did Thomas Alva Edison own from his idea of plugging a utensil into a receptacle of electric energy?…(before such things even existed?)

Wealth of his creative exploration far exceeded wealth of his bank account simply because it brought so much to situation of contribution by rational organic. That opened so much creative thinking that it actually led into and foretold the great opportunity of eventual/past/future citizen of the Fifth.

Mr. Edisons "unveiling" and "harnessing" of a fundamental form of potential becoming kinetic,…. energy,…. created by movement of charged particles such as electrons, positrons or ions, brought a clean, natural manifestation of light and heat and diverse applications of work moment and mobility. One may assure T.A. Edison's position as a citizen of the Fifth.

What of potential of "soul?" Like smart atom in "potentia" it is no-where, no-when and not in occurrence or reoccurrence. It is Dark and not present.

Yet it, according to itself and reiterated by all other souls,… falls into realization. Not corporeal and yet apparently "felt" by rational organic, time limit of this very unique idea is, like recognition of smart atom,… rationality itself.

Rational organic unveils and recognizes harness-like possession of soul, smart atom and work moment.

Soul of/with rationality being fractal tendril of Dark chaos.

Smart atom of/with rationality being primary tool of corporality.

Work moment of/with rationality being opportunity of contribution.

113

Within this absolutely fundamental system and its probable commonality the Feynman's and Edison's cultivated hadras of imagination for each significant point of manifestation. Citizen of the Fifth knows and understands "potential" and will not brush over it in favor of manipulating "alpha-animal" hierarchy of in-tribe.

"Prayer is supreme act of creative imagination. Dark epiphany of rationality for rationality and recognition of soul, smart atom and work. The "one" prayer is accomplished by Dark chaos realm of all possibility, becoming visible to heart organ, (soul) and projecting "image," the receptacle (separate containment) that is "being" of worship as presence in measure of its capacity. (adapted from: preface Harold Bloom, Bollingen series XCI, Princeton/ 1997)

That image is "belief" in unit of "self." Internal strength of soul vent and peripheral incorporeal mortar component holding "brick" in place. "Aura of self" sustains presence, location, unit contribution and identity. All of this hails from a dreamy, vague gravity of belief.

Brick, as smart atom is primary tool of corporality. (well-known lyric: all we are is just another brick in the wall) It is very well defined and as such easy to believe in. Yet those who would journey to extreme limits of familiarity suggest that "manifest" display of this basic, fundamental actually comes into question. It becomes "fuzzy" and the best way of describing it is as product of probability made manifest or localized by observation.

This idea sounds somewhat dreamy and vague and may actually suggest that principle tool of corporality is "only" defined by belief in observation of it. Frequency of occurrence, or incidence is also so short against Dark chaos background, that it falls into a category of "uncertainty." Of all creatures, the rational is the only one that may truly be uncertain.

Image of self as "being" of worship in a presence of measurable capacity, ….a display across an entire minute corner of fractal chaos extrapolation,….may be a humbling revelation of identity as fertile dirt soil contribution of cosmic fodder.

But for Dark soul vent, rationality may only be necessary but expendable ingredient that makes a system or scheme work. Realization that is carried with rationality, as short, or uncertain, or limited, or dreamy as it is, is still localized within work moment and effects presentation of smart atom. Contribution is that realization and in that recognition is creation of one single cosmos. Coming into existence of such a cosmos creates rational organic which will embellish Dark chaos by contributing energy of such a distinguishable duplicity.

Strength is in simplicity of perpetuity principle. This allows that such a system be common and routine on the great Dark chaos map of potential point creation.

Rationality has given itself a precious gift of soul vent. It is a very unique situation of direct access and association with ultimate creative initiative. In fact, it is a tiny piece of that chaos reservoir in "possession" of rational organic unit. It empowers the "one" and moves it to an acceptance that all other "ones" are also in this "possession." A beautiful gift of companionship with an entire cosmos of souls may be decisive in "lifting" rational organic out of a somewhat mundane, animal belief in occurrence as only "fodder."

Daring to also acknowledge the organic aspect as just a necessary but expendable ingredient is not a far-fetched idea.

Contribution has been made in rationality that holds creative force (God) within, as ownership of said force and as such unique in all of creation. It is very advantageous for "each" organic unit and "each" cosmic unit in maintaining time-line and spacial organization beyond self, as that organic aspect will age and die.

"Key" descriptive here is "each." One of the ones in common and routine experience that marks point creation on the Chaos map like twinkling stars in a great, Dark night.

If the old saying, "as above, so below" is still acceptable then familiar stellar cosmic map may be "below" aspect of unlimited point creations twinkling into and out of existence within a much larger, yet still fundamental idea. This point of view may be a necessary ingredient in imagination of a citizen of the Fifth.

Matrix of such an extremely large extrapolation is of course still well within chaos of everything/forever. A "matrix" is,...."situation or circumstance that allows or encourages origin, development and growth."

(Encarta world Dictionary)

What if familiar stellar map is "identical" to point creation on Dark chaos map? That might suggest an eerie type of descendent "order" in Dark chaos reservoir and directive of point-creation by perpetuity principle. That would mean that Holy Trinity is following a "pattern" in activating creations.

What if familiar stellar map "is" point creation on Dark chaos map? That might suggest that all dimensions of time, space and localization coming into being, contributing and dying out are /can be realized in manifestation before/in front of awareness of rationality.

Why would that not be possible when "all" possibility is available from Dark chaos, a tendril of which is "possession" of each rational organic.

Is the short, uncertain, dreamy localization privy to unlimited force of all of creation always, even though it is unfathomable and incomprehensible? Dark is beyond understanding but point creation and hence cosmic evolution are graspable by rationality due to familiar example at hand. It might even make sense that if one exists in creation then all creation should be available even if process toward and understanding of is not within ability to do so.

If such extreme energy conviction cannot be "rationalized" then approach toward process and understanding must be pursued from tendril of Dark chaos. One might suggest that within that fractal extrapolation of Dark is a very, possibly equally large potential of imagination. It would be within an imaginative soul that citizen of the Fifth must search. Unveiling "reason" for/of rational organic and its direction and fate may be at hand.

Richard Feynman:….."the reason why a complete description of the corporeal has not been described is that the ones entertaining and involving themselves with this great endeavor have not yet developed enough imagination."

Involving "self" with such a volume of soul would definitely form a significant well-spring of spiritual identity. Taking self to that water-shed to sip a cool, Dark depth of that creative potential may bring "relief" to the complex fever of phenomenal status-quo. Similar to "beautitude" this identity may be realized as a "gate" or "dock" for commerce of a creative elaboration. This would be a usable, functioning entrance/exit that is labeled as such and path to it must be found and known. It is not a place to linger, as identity may be mysteriously misplaced, but enjoying a ladle of pristine Dark creative potentiality may be what the revered shaman suggested. A fortunate result may be learning to, "live freely within light."

In fact, "purpose" of the Fifth may simply be to acquire this state of being. It is of course a creative civilization without borders, barriers, limits, creed, greed, color, or animal hierarchy. It is citizenry keeping self and passion vital and flexible by always recognizing its ties with all other disciplines, studies and devotions. (Herman Hesse, Magister Ludi) It is a not-so-much tongue in cheek,...utopian society,.... worthy of interaction with one of the other ones.

Though act of such an involvement may be impossible state of worthiness could be admirably broadcast. That does not really do anything for an alternative rational organic, contributing in its own sense, different from a possibility of interaction and "uncertain" of its own situation.

Using the word "pride" is not appropriate (too animal) but in seeking of "dock" as beautitude a forth-with beacon of "satisfaction" from familiar rationality of the Fifth, may be worn as an epaulet,..... perhaps marking a civilization with a highly coveted gold or silver braid.

Again, bridge may be in a hard wire "design" that will not allow interacting ones, but why not "show" or "display" such an evolved citizenry.

Still uncertain, vulnerable, perhaps harboring minute animal tendency, but in a vortex of creative function a coveted gold braid will announce a truly advantageous situation of understanding and with no obligation, forward a potential involvement.

As above? There may be a very simple reason why that particular attitude of a civilization has never been realized,....because it has never been described accurately.

Average rational situation involves some exploration but really not that much further than a TV remote. The most back-assed jungle village now has at least twelve channels and anything half developed, a mirage of reality TV.

Description of situation of rational organic and its position/location relative to Dark chaos sea/reservoir of all possibility will be described.

A true citizen of the Fifth will recognize and begin to understand it. This will happen because of an intense exploration into a realm of imagination. To create this description is one thing but it is project of the Fifth to find and understand it. It will eradicate action of reaching for a remote and replace it with the remote.

Recognize wispy vulnerability of silken thread of spider's web reflecting light against a Dark thunderstorm. Completely exposed to a barrage of wind from every direction and rain with potential to rip and tear tendril, it never-the-less endures a power beyond its minute, almost random presence.

It holds tenaciously to an equally battered leaf, describing them both with location though still extremely susceptible to a great rage of chaos. If the storm increases its mayhem then they may possibly relinquish that identity and disperse into fundamental fragments of a molecular or even atomic debris from which they came.

But if the storm whose velocity they are somewhat familiar with, and perhaps even designed to endure does its usual and then abates, then this tendril may be elongated to a more advantageous position or in fact other smaller tendrils may be added, then beginning to describe an interdependent, almost "family" of vulnerable tendrils hoping and holding tenaciously to leaf.

Of course ability to hunt, (pursue satisfaction) and aspect of companionship forming more bonding with leaf, as well as probable increased odds of endurance and survival may allow the relaxing of a guard, that stands by always ready to repair or rebuild if possible. (that perhaps being idea, confidence and belief of "self")

Such a network of tendrils bonded into "family" of support and co-operation can grow into possibility of a "nation" of web and purpose.

Wow, awesome confidence and security and a beautiful shimmering of golden epaulet displaying wealth and resistance against all that would try to damage it. The web catches morning dew and is lubricated by it. Strength in elasticity and tolerance increases its attractiveness and it becomes a mecca for the less strong. Tendrils from everywhere arrive to join up and pursue their own version of satisfaction. A "nation" web is strong and sure, but for those other pesky "nation" webs and their versions of satisfaction.

That may be the stand-off of generations of webs. Some satisfied but in defense and others hoping for satisfaction and in attack. (by any means violent or not, perhaps even in submission) (still very effective, just refer to the tactics of Mahatma Gandhi) So, ...this may become focus and obsession, ... but perhaps "nation" webs have forgotten about the great Dark storm. Such an entangled chaos of energy from beyond comprehension of web-remote presence, can and will rattle that cage of filaments to point of potential disengagement.

A web "civilization" may present and even broadcast location but it would be a tricky situation for one web civilization to detach from their leaf and drift in possibly quite violent circumstance to arrive at, recognize and at almost a most extreme opportunity,.... bond with web civilization of a familiar wispy vulnerable silken thread of same chaotic thunderstorm.

That would not even be taking into consideration an unlimited number of thunderstorms. Such a wispy, vulnerable silken thread in a Dark chaos maelstrom holding at one end onto leaf and at the other onto be-leaf certainly sounds like a temporary, or perhaps temporal situation.

It is, and must be. Contribution cannot continue uninterrupted. Individual thread, or family of threads, or nation of threads should be defined within and by civilization of threads. (or is that the other way around)

Short, uncertain, limited and dreamy silk can still claim miniscule interior of said filament,...... that being soul vent of all possibility,.... as possession.

That leads to action of "will have been done." Or is the saying "will, having been done," or simply a modal verb phrase indicating a temporality not yet acquired. (future perfect) Diction, syntax and grammar are like beautitude and spiritual identity best offered as a "gate" or "dock" in and from which extreme creative imagination may be visualized within capacity of being.

Soul vent of all possibility within silken thread, tenaciously hanging on to a shuddering leaf, itself perhaps adversely effected by "family" and "nations" of tendrils, is susceptible to a constant barrage of chaos creativity storm, (in fact it is part of) ….. but surprisingly enough resisting it in fear of not absorbing it,……. but being absorbed by it.

Few are the pilgrims of Homeric path,….. that which does not offer recognition or wealth but "only" satisfaction in display.

Focus and obsession in "satisfaction" of nation webs that engross presence in an almost random situation of vulnerability, …..forgotten or never known,….. the great Dark chaos maelstrom accepts prayer of rationality thanking chaos for ability of specialization.

This is a great gift of complementarity at the level of smart atom, particle/wave theory, light, gravity and Dark energy.

This great gift of prayer as a means of existence and a "causing to exist," is supreme act of creative imagination. By virtue of "sharing" the unknown aspires to be known and unveiled "image" manifests as fragile, vulnerable receptacle of worshiper's being. (adapted from Harold Bloom; preface Bollingen series XCI/ Princeton press 1997)

A citizen must not fear being absorbed for it will happen regardless but should attempt to absorb what is possible in measure of capacity while still involved in/with identity of their creative prayer.

Symbiosis across Dark straights and harbors and reflections in hour glass narrows, are always a mutually beneficial relationship. Utilizing "dock" and "gate" of each and all, beautitude and spiritual well as well as binary manifest aspects of pseudo phenomenal. Complimentarity, causing, sharing, image and unveiling,….even principle of uncertainty,… are all part of description of familiar rational organic and its position relative to Dark chaos reservoir. Perpendicularly overlapped and vertically entangled, rotated and fractally extrapolated,…. location is of course all and none of the above. That in itself is a sameness that suggests profit from connection. Commerce and trade may be,...... as previously offered an extreme fundamental of "reason" for perpetuity principle.

Sameness is routine and that is success of Holy trinity as action of creation ensemble. One might look to an interval and listen between.

Click,...click, click was heard by mature citizen as it foraged in scrub of manifest mundane. Rationality cricket was warning of a soul predator. This audible was an abrasive friction that chirped out an alarm across dunes of civilization. Intermingled with and almost indistinguishable from chatter of vertebrates were signals of ancient principles.

A young pledge was being "positioned" and the drawing was on twenty billion years of an un-acknowledgeable. Idea was hunt yet trophy of self, tribe, nation and civilization was only the spiritual scent of a space between. Further was not possible but to just be in range with a net of compassion may be submission that is necessary in recognizing a predator as parent of soul.

A ruthlessly aggressive, not by inclination but by sheer power, fundamental of soul as chaos filament brings with it, a determined persistence of hunt. At point of capture compassionate arrow is directed just as deity submits to recognition. Most see a different situation but when entertaining concepts of the Fifth a relinquishing of energy for the material and then a material contribution to energy is a "timely" device. It may illustrate a binary "sharing" of presence, (civilization) and therefore displays in temporality.

A citizen must appreciate the difference. In absence of light there is a Darkness where things go bump and click in that great night. They, citizens should be the ones that go bump and click back.

That amount of creative ability is now and previous and tomorrow.

Imagination is escape of limiting rationally mundane and by such, a purposeful decision as to indulge in the unlimited, may a bridge, gate, or dock be made available.

Access to that "soul food" should bring an otherworld "nutrition" into a creative process. Citizen should be digesting every available morsel.

It is a huge contribution and embellishment and will begin scheme of an advantageous situation of awareness and with no obligation forward or display an exceptionally evolved citizenry.

In a choosing to embrace creative imagination (as described by an ancient Sufi sage) phenomenal energy of contribution may actually be unveiled, as in Hadras of presence, and a true "designer" of the Fifth will arrive at "involvement within process of being."

It cannot be left in or taken out of the hand of a creation singularity because it is a collaboration or sharing. Energy of released arrow is in absolute synchronicity with submission of Dark chaos reservoir of all possibility. Again likened to hero/heroin on the hunt. Surviving and enduring in simplicity of that moment is "familiar" and excelling in it is attainable yet requires an unrelenting persistence of soul searching and application.

Of course, the searching part is more common than application and that is because it is easier. Method is required in order to fulfil purpose and although vision of dream may present, it may require a "Mother Teresa" type of commitment of method in order to achieve.

Sharing is of necessity an unveiling and that may be forwarded as a communion in method of rational organic tending to realize ebb and flow. A river that flows past point does indeed involve a variable current. One may have said that it is either in or out, off or on and that is still valid containing variance.

Resistance against river is "identity" but any new step does not carry that with. Flow is different at any particular point. Each is a situation of one single occasion of resistance. That may be why any one of the ones may be spirited off in an incomprehensible direction, never to be capable of a realization of alien point creation. Option may be in plurality beyond speculation.

That does not suggest that one is prohibited from imaginative realization of "concept" of other point creation and that may be fulfilment of a maturing citizen of the Fifth.

Suppose that Dark chaos maelstrom of all possibility has via soul filament of self an approaching energy storm of imagination. At a distance, it may appear as though they were interacting yet due to extreme capability of vitality in both, they must by unrelenting incompatible qualities of sameness on different frontiers, remain at arms-length. It is an in-between and not a place where identity would venture. Perhaps better to pass by, realize circumstance only for what it resembles and not dwell on that unique appearance. In case of an evolving citizen such approaches become more common yet for "time in being" simply forwarding acknowledgement of this "strangement" having occurred in imaginative tendril of soul filament of Dark creation,........may have to suffice.

Then there are those true soul gypsies. Ones who clearly feel like that is enough temporal monotony. Perhaps a poet walking the crest of a dune on the Namibe with a great desert on his right and a great sea on his left. (would he be heading North?) It may have to be just such a gypsy to be the one who could not simply let it be any longer.

This is Horton, an elephant from the amazing Dr. Seuss stories and of course Dr. Seuss himself. This is the one "who" that hears click in a vast Dark and clicks back. Perhaps this is an unrelenting pachyderm who after receiving a "bump" marches, or struggles, or crawls with "Mother Teresa" commitment of method, in order to achieve and finally bump back.

Relatively speaking a bump from an elephant should be quite noticeable yet such extreme imagination can only be recognized by citizens who are struggling to do so.

As in this amazing story, the rationally mundane will scoff at an oversized declaration of alternative and may even isolate or chastise the hero/herione. Usually that is OK and seeker can ignore a tragically boring society. But it is they that cannot ignore citizen "who" who pursues almost imperceptible situation. As standoff of disbelief and stubborn tenacity builds to a threatening crescendo it would have to be imaginative alternative itself that declares its validity and much to the humbling surprise of rationality a new level of awareness is introduced.

This is at a maturing Fifth civilization and with no obligation it forwards or displays the beginning of an exceptionally evolved citizenry.

A great aboriginal sage from the Manitoulin describes "Fifth River Running.".......'Serpents come from Darkness reaching out to tap a soul. They are tendrils of a chaos storm luring rational possession into an ever variable oneness of creation." (adaptation)

Those who would be hero/heroin of final civilization should perhaps not camp so high up a bank but might want to move closer to the raging current. It is not a cautious way but a lot may be learned from torrent before inevitable submergence. Some would simply call it,.......living closer to the edge."

That imaginative alternative is after all, not on its bank but in Dark tumultuous maelstrom.

There was a speaking about unrelenting incompatible qualities of sameness on different frontiers. Can or should one interpret this as a polarity boundary? The simple will always endure. Is it similar to a repulsing positive/positive of electromagnetics on a much more fantastic yet identical scale? Perhaps the energy field of a planet relative to either and both the needle of a compass and a galaxial vitality?

The phrase was "that it may be necessary to remain at arms-length" and that perhaps identity would not venture into that virga. Rational organic might "learn" to be able to imagine idea without of course indulging or interacting with it.

It is surely a trickier situation to sit on a bank while one's feet are testing a numbing extemporaneous then to be high on a phenomenal shore with said appendages feeling a warmth of clearly defined bonfire.

"Coming to know" of idea may follow method of display that presents in a runic/alphabetical/language with very ancient connections. The old English/Germanic is "leornian." It is from an Indo-European word meaning "track" which also produced English "lore" and "last."

The underlying idea is to follow a course of instruction." (Encarta World Dictionary) One may follow "track" in either direction, kind of like an entropy arrow. But doesn't this all sound familiar? (track, lore, endure)

It does because it is part of sameness of incompatible, unrelenting quality of energies on different frontiers. Track is left with purpose of finding. A shaman on the arctic tundra sameness sees a distant Dark wolf cross his path. He knows this presentation is pure Magik. He approaches track and knows that following one way should produce a wolf but he chooses to follow it the other, to the reason for primal sorcery that presented it.

KiiJay finds the reason and takes her home to his snow hut. There they begin a great journey that exorcizes her diseased lie, reunites herself with brother and mother and moves them all toward the birth of a great savior.

Learning suggestion of a Magik track places a citizen in the moccasins of a powerful shaman. It may be beginning of intense spiritual adventure fueled by a powerful imagination that is not "limited" by a rationally mundane.

Physics is usually not associated with Magik yet that is basically what Richard Feynman suggested in saying that,… "the reason why the phenomenal has not yet been fully described is that those physicists doing the work do not yet have sufficient imagination."

When every citizen is wearing shaman snow-shoes they will not and cannot fall into a depth of trivial, material consumerism to wallow helplessly in a shallow rationality of acquisition greed and social position. Nor even to be so professionally submerged that the sqweek of an inquiring child or shout of a population of "who's" living on a dust speck on a clover will not be heard.

Every citizen of the Fifth will be a Horton and a powerful aura of imagination will replace status quo and surround and saturate every rational organic, opening ideas of new and greater possibilities.

In such a circumstance of open mind and open soul limiting, locking feelings of fear and mistrust may give way to a great unveiling of compassion and a true definition of fair energetic commerce and trade will be on display.

Finding ways of distribution for plentiful resources of a trembling leaf to which the fragile rational web is attached and protecting vulnerability of said leaf may be an honorable occupation of a new-age artisan.

Every opportunity of experiencing manifest phenomenal fulfils contribution and thus purpose. In description of emerging citizen may be included idea of a qualitative meaning, exemplifying and therefore benefiting an embellishment of rationality as presence.

Any one such opportunity should not find itself in the following position.

"There are rational organics traveling from one conference to another and are convinced that in doing so that something is really happening and that they have accomplished something; whereas in reality they have shirked the labor of true contribution and now seek refuge in a great deal of idle talk for their helplessness." (adapted from "History of the Concept of Time" by Martin Heidegger)

All of this complex meandering is giving way to more complex meandering and there are those who feel like they are contributing by inventing more and more trivial ways of complex meandering. They are actually getting monetarily rich and wealthy in social status by expanding the demeaning practices of insignificant use of time.

There must be a "method" out there to turn the tide of this meaningless trend of embarrassment. Does anyone still know how to read?

So for a time, citizens of the Fifth civilization of humankind might have to walk track of Homeric path with few pilgrim travelers at their side. It has been way of the past and may continue for generations. Yet another beacon goes out into that great night and with it perhaps a way of skipping over fallow fields to fertility that lies further along.

Never-the-less permission has been granted to engage creative expression of the Fifth and within foundation of this encounter of existence and being,...... fulfillment may be a necessary consequence.

Earlier discussion of members of the Fifth from the past might not want to be forgotten. Citizen that is engaged never walks alone even when without company and the Fifth is an ageless civilization and not particularly based on participatory volume, but on a qualitative criteria. They are true hero/heroin who simply acknowledge, contribute and pass and they are the "ones" who have understood that as one of the ones in a single opportunity of participation they have taken "care" of that responsibility.

Being Dasein is always incomplete and in condition of no contribution outstanding circumstance itself is no longer. In reaching of "wholeness" aloneness of situation is concluded without identity. Accordingly, as mature principle it cannot be understood in pre-possession. It is basis of its own "kind" of being. (again adapted from Martin Heidegger)

At point creation a "type" of existence was described in a progressive star sequence eventually resulting in rational organic. It took a long time and became quite complex. It was/is very unique but unlike principles of religious dogma declares as only one of the ones. Simplicity of process is alarming in a fundamental give and take. It may, almost absurdly be a minute harbor of commerce just next to a random Dark chaos maelstrom of possibility.

Within this tiny harbor,.... gates, docks and perhaps bridges are necessary as intermediary necessities of doing commerce. Mostly, as in phenomenal port locations they are not noticed in a flurry of activity. In understanding a limited time involved in transaction, critical necessity of placement and removal of these intermediaries is a fundamental.

Where is that responsibility? It lies with gate, dock and bridge builder. The ones that move necessary means of providing exchange and sharing of commerce. Perhaps the one that only focuses directly upon that responsibility and not much else. It would be appropriate. This situation may involve "action." It is not response.

Which "who" is capable of that? Even Horton "responded" to the tiny voice of a who. So, it may have been up to professor "who" to build the bridge that may or may not create a sharing or commerce of relation. This was done without any knowledge of a sharing or possible commerce of relation.

The old saying may be "going out on a limb." How does that work?

He/she just reached out and took it in a grasp, without foresight. How does that occur?

Perhaps by having an intention of occurrence.

That is a suggestion of action and creates realm of situation. It may be creation formula of rationality. Like opposed digits of metacarpals searching for manipulative advantage, eventually leading to space flight and pollution, that function/analogy may be a valid pursuit of Fifth description result.

Are the ones in house?.....not parallel but overlapping perpendicular and vertically entangled, rotated and fractally extrapolated?

Then their arrives, always arrives a miniscule one that only focuses directly upon that bridge building responsibility.

From Holy trinity to intent, a blink in a cosmic realm with no time, then a very brief moment and then the light goes out. Civilizations have come and gone and contribution has been made. Identity has been forgotten but for unlimited possibilities of concept of identity and perhaps an intention of occurrence. (really,… unlimited possibilities of concept of identity)

Can it be true that "time" is the only meaningful currency of trade and commerce between chaos storm and quaint inner harbor of rationality. It is the only situation when circumstance may be measured and contribution confirmed. Of course, this has all been suggested in religious dogma and a result of such a "weighing in" declared loud and clear.

All are "familiar" but for impossibility in all realms, local and alien, of ones capable of continued "identity." That is not possible. Only contribution will continue and that is meaningful because of time contribution,…situation contribution or contribution of energy embellishment.

Like opposed digits of metacarpals searching for manipulative advantage. Strong enough to hold yet not so strong as to break. How is that known, either in divine belief or rational experience? Was it perhaps trial and error? With so much "time" available (not individual but collective) could that "grip" have perhaps faltered a few thousand times before just a correct "pressure" was learned to manipulate the egg without breaking or dropping it?

It may sound too simple but cradling of rationality might have occurred in a cumulative effort rather than a dropped egg that was caught with just the correct force. Certainly, opposed digits would have helped but it may still be a bit extravagant to assume that something so fragile could have landed on a complex organic to make it a rational organic.

Perhaps better to accept the idea that through many eras rational situation was growing out of circumstance governed by instinct and appetite and that across favorable complex organic life sustaining stability of environment that reasonable or logical or knowledgeable or even emotional criteria began to display in a sensible operating "method."

An idea that this was "learned" certainly contradicts "divine creation" theory. (dropped egg)

A cosmic blink with no time when complex organic was developing toward a receptacle capable of "containing" and to a certain extent being contained by a "frame of mind and soul" would have been period of having "intention of rational occurrence."

Some might say that intent would have had to have been there at point creation. Yet one might offer that perhaps billions of situations that occurred in stellar evolution did not get to an intention of rational organic. Is there a point, place, situation or circumstance where idea of rationality becomes viable and a plan or purpose of development toward reciprocating contribution becomes an influence of change?

A dropped egg theory would again say, sure it is now, but maybe there is a significant grey area when the egg is rolled around and broken or picked up for a bit and broken or stepped on and broken.

This may be a reality of rationality. The more one may ponder presence, the more that it appears in a realm of random suggestion. As it is grounded in and an intimate corner of chaos, so does the "nature" of such circumstance suggest a roll of dice with intent.

Sometimes it works and sometimes it doesn't. Responsibility of that incremental access toward commerce of energy reciprocals may indeed lie with a gate or dock builder. He/she introduces "beautitude."

The intro of such allowing a continually enhanced gate of chaos cauldron of possibility,….forever enriched by all forms of aesthetic donation,…beyond awe, worth and excellence and in that process, absolutely complete in function without beginning or end.

At face value it may indeed sound "Godly" yet this is not activity of amazing processes but only description. This is a rope ladder gingerly suspended over a monstrous chasm. It is indeed a bridge/gate between a dark chaos maelstrom and a precariously authorized rationality that is in the tender grasp of each hero/heroin on a road trip toward the Fifth. Perhaps this is finest of spider soul filament that drifts across the storm until finding anchorage on a particular leaf and maturing into rationality.

It may be sketchy at best and in realm of Holy Trinity that is probably standard. In dealing with an unbelievable, inconceivable vitality that contains every unimaginable and perhaps a few "familiar" possibilities and a tiny harbor of transaction with very limited "operatum temporalis" the idea might be to accept description only as a walkway and not look to carry too much baggage. At a future perfect situation, a more fortified dock may be realized, when gravity of that great responsibility may be accepted as firmly as gravity ashore. (position of the Fifth where that "will have been done")

Modern rational opinion is very much taken for granted as a bubble that is completely full. How can one increase lights on, and values, beliefs and techniques based on logical, explicable principles? (Encarta)

It is a closed system. Causality of a tiny "who" bridge builder cannot ever be found within system. It would be an amount of potency, Magik and tenacity of imaginative capacity which may "cause" and that would be influenced by a great desire and intent though within a vacuum of "outside information." Without slipping from this narrow walkway a professor "who" must continue to climb over, around and even through the bubble, learning its bulging enthusiasm, debilitating depressions and worm holes that intricately interlace themselves willy-nilly throughout the ethereal, precariously authorized fragility of its substance.

If the thin membrane is broken contents will simply disperse throughout Dark chaos, so "knowing" of rational bubble and understanding of a manipulation process would be imperative "method" of a one tiny "who" with a great commitment/promise.

As in the story of Horton, part of "method" of a professor may be in design of their contraption. As in design of many members of the Fifth who have walked the Homeric path a runic/alphabetical abstraction of letter representation has been a significant part of their contraption.

It has been available for so many eras but is beginning to lose credibility to "easier" educational/media tools.

One may believe that message that is delivered more quickly may be forgotten more quickly.

It may be remembered that in Jay Griffith's "Pip Pip," (Harper Collins/ 99) that an ancient venerated sage Kundera once spoke that "there is a secret bond between slowness and memory, between speed and forgetting." Whiteledge,…"fast talking and fast visuals promote fast thought" it may not be best but it is first, "slower knowledge is shared, crosses disciplines and is flexible." Ivan Illich,…."tell me how fast you go and I will tell you who you are." An aggressive appetite for change actually offers monotony of sameness. All airports are pretty much the same.

Interestingly enough, though system of delivery has surpassed any standard of acceleration message has not. That, perhaps being an advance of triviality and "wasted time." Yes, it is valid that all phenomenal experience is contribution but there might be a qualitative criterion associated with investigation of rational bubble and possibility of a slight increase in its diameter or radius. Giogordo Bruno and so many others have tried intense focus of expansion but if other rational organic bubbles are not ready for intervention of a new larger one the result may be a sizzling pop!

If message requires a knowledgeable basis of understanding and is delivered with Pythagorean subtlety then perhaps it has a chance of "sinking in." A format that allows going back a bit to re-evaluate previously delivered information might also be a benefit. All of this could very well be part of the contraption of a hero/professor "who" diligently working away at building a tiny bridge/gate that offers "beautitude" and beyond.

Incremental expansion may not even be measurable on a daily basis but like the pyramids and Great Wall, construction involved one brick at a time and especially in this case the all-important mortar was accumulating as well and holding structure together.

Mortar in a stylized account being an intangible, holding place and defining separate moment. Perhaps similar to brick as familiar of rationality bubble. A fragile membrane that maintains limit of individual perception. In physics, ultimate edge of common sense would be "relic" cosmic background radiation at periphery of phenomenal. At this temporal extreme, undulations may be present that fluctuate with ability to observe. Such a limit does not occur without "stuff" of rationality. (time, distance, velocity, gravity, etc.) Those measurable qualities contribute to "aura of self" supporting and sustaining presence, relative location and embellishment by unit of identity.

It carries gravity of belief though there is no absolute proof of existence. (like "Horton Hears a Who," that would have to arrive from outside of system.) Frequency and duration of occurrence of one rational bubble is so short that it may necessarily fall into the category of "uncertainty."

In physics quantum uncertainty principle holds that position and momentum of a particle (flawed atom) cannot be determined at the same time moment. This would be similar to stating that perception of rational brick bubble is authorized by an intangible and that it is that same void of unseen mortar that allows for structure of pyramid, wall and bridge that facilitates commerce of existing and of contribution. (in both physical realm of conscious work moment and imaginative realm of Dark soul energy)

Mortar holds brick in place. It is an intangible that defines separate moment, similar to "placement" of brick or rational bubble. As spiritual-rational bubble-brick has its place in pyramid, so does personally possessive moment of individuality.

All units, by divine formula create embellishment that is pyramid in the middle of equilibrium desert.

When Horton's time moment and the "who's" time moment were both recognized within relative positions and their momentum of interaction was stabilized the uncertainty of their existence was eliminated. (and of course at the very end a tiny dust speck falls onto professors "who's" lap and he hears a tiny voice)

So, one might assume that there is a fragile rationality egg that drops into possession or is learned manipulation. From energy and matter arrives diametrical opposites as a new concept of perhaps a synergy of blood as soul filament and flawed smart atom of material. It will hatch and soar into and to some extent master the phenomenal. Adventure has been somewhat impressive and dreams reach far into limits of familiar manifest.

Arching down from a spiritual high of dominating so much natural leaf function there may in suggesting transcendence of duality, suddenly arise re-realization of a three-phase ingestion/absorption of soul, as Dark chaos blood of possibility. This is very fundamental. It may take one back to Holy Trinity of gravity wave trigger,…effecting pressure reservoir,…to create point.

It is described in the Alchemical Wedding of Christian Rosenkreutz (as adapted in the above) and is offered to all pilgrim citizens of the Fifth.

Presenting from beneath a phenomenal veil, soul filament, like ashes of a Phoenix, swells passion of the Fifth to engulf fragile rational egg that had allowed its creation.

Ingestion involves enjoying royal patronage of rationality as result/sponsor of evolution, allowing ancient theory of a primal situation dominated by serpents, (chaos entanglement) and an avian magistrate (pre-rational organic) that co-incidentally must be sacrificed in process of egg incarnation.

All adapted from (The Alchemical wedding of C.R.)

So, the unique spiritual is visibly respected in lower vehicle of citizen and that is awareness of Holy Trinity as fundamental of perpetuity principle. With knowledge of creation supreme individual is no longer in position of "uncertainty" for intervention from outside of rationality has interceded on behalf of gnosis. Purpose of experience may be nothing more than "living freely within light." That develops imagination and that forms more significant contribution. That embellishes equilibrium desert of chaos vitality with a very obvious, meaningful pyramid of "having occurred" and that allows sand coming out of a time narrows to sparkle just a little bit brighter then sand going in. Change is of the Homeric path and is effect in heart and soul of citizen.

Just exactly what is a pyramid in the middle of a great equilibrium desert? It may be a very short period of order within chaos. (perhaps associated with a fractal extrapolation) As such its possibility was/is/will always be available. It was made from chaos and is a part of chaos. If a desert wanderer encounters such a structure, questions must arise,….. what and why primarily,….. and secondarily,…..how?

Why,....perhaps to embellish random possibility with direction and therefore purpose. (why reason?.... as extreme basis of growth)

What,.....always a perplexing question,....only a dedicated nomad would assign the "time" necessary for an answer.

How,... tools must be available within chaos but probably cannot be directly used by rationality.

A sad truth is that most nomads would go around it, attribute some God quality and carry on. Moderns struggle with the "who" of great creativity but that may be diversion of self-glorification. Even Gods themselves offer that simplified fixation. However,.... it was made from dirt fodder of common possibility. (not to be confused with dirt fodder of uncommon possibility)

Intangible mortar of rationality forms "shape" of dirt/fodder possibility which simultaneously in turn offers potential of rationality. As was previously suggested a chicken was sacrificed in order to bring forth an egg. (so much for the age old question)

Oddly, or obviously enough, these are criteria of "entanglement theory." (as in primal situation dominated by serpents) Information "about" an operative systematic situation (rationality) is obscured in process of being observed. Citizen might not want to quantify circumstance as that observation will probably collapse variables into premature "fixations" or "limits" that may hinder placement of brick/bubble in mortar assisted construction of an observation with few elementals at point and gradually increasing elementals at opposite platform.

At this auspicious moment, it may be necessary to quote a venerable Persian sage. Ibn¢ Arabi,.... "the perpetual existentiation of possibilities is an area of pure discontinuity. Recurrence of like but not same."

One might have a look at what one "has" in order to determine what one might "have." This may be basic "admit one" ticket to the Fifth. Is it OK to reduce such a Holy possession to such an absolute common denominator? Each ticket has exactly the same "value."

If a dirt/fodder potency becomes dirt/fodder capacity and common denominator is augmented and enriched as a possession, this may "cause" according to desire and intent in a pure and lucid superiority of self, pushing deeper into creation.

Accepting ownership of the most fundamental properties of creation (matter and energy) allows the "has" group to "have" a future perfect confidence.

Is there a slightly higher? (more qualitative) aspect in pyramid capsule-nodule of pressure energy bundles in general homeostasis of chaos energy reservoir? Can those near a membrane of cosmic background radiation be affected by gravity rent to induce a miniscule fracture of now enriched and just a little bit more sparkling point creation?

Of billions of point bursts of imaginative existence will some mature toward "purpose" of a rational situation and fulfil a cosmic destiny? Will "reason" of accumulated star dust recognize, accept and push into necessary consequence of work moment with advantage?

These are not questions open for discussion in the Fifth civilization. Entering the Fifth assigns that responsibility. It cannot be ignored and "time" will be given for such a realm of creation. (this is valid, ..."time" will be given to a true citizen of the Fifth) Possibilities will be unveiled from chaos/soul reservoir with tools of imagination. Methods of manipulating this egg-like manifest are as varied as ability to visualize, at first in fourth Hadra of the incorporeal, idea images having form but in subtle immaterial. Then arriving in dense, visible, audible and sensible and these characteristics and disciplines are as variable as any entire rational realm.

Imagination is of course even involved in questioning of rationality. Feynman was quite accurate in stating that knowledge of physics of a cosmos will not proceed without greater imagination. This is a "causing to appear" of the gnostic heart. Delving into chaos soul filament of perpendicular opposed, overlapping, entanglement of energy and matter might require utmost command of subject and absolute flexibility in interaction of alternative disciplines and passions of still common possibilities.

One definition of "science" is,....."something studied or performed methodically." Would it be improper to say "science of imagination?"

135

Once one has crossed boundaries of the imaginable in a still limited context a calm spirit may move into empowering revelation. Will that herald introduction of a technique or "scientific method" to pass beyond those borders and re-define/interpret pyramid nodule? If duplicated in independent circumstance "method" may prove valid.

At moment of identity possession there is an almost immediate fear of losing it. Complicated spirits deal with it via a number of safeguards but pure soul will not ignore, cover or hide, but indulge in it. The homogenous pulse of being will be accentuated by an exclamation mark of actuality.

This is self of citizen being uniquely distinguished from civilization. A student of the Fifth will be seen and will have an address.

Recognition brings responsibility and goal might be to know how and when to direct magnitude of this exceptional vision. Many a sensei and prophet have donated lifetimes in obtaining a matter/energy balance with which a citizen of the Fifth begins their journey.

Citizen will be nourished by ying/yang, plus/minus and duality of rational organic position, and in that feeding will move camp not so far up the bank from chaos river and thus closer to its essential message.

Meditating on a moonlit pyra-node, a committed vitality may feel a sort of quiver or shiver that authenticates possibility plasma. It may be just a minute tremor with a hint of preponderance. It is an immeasurable, illuminating a transcendent fractal extrapolation at periphery of void. This will be the only moment when a citizen can glimpse soul.

Hence, they must raise beacon of self in and from a chaos sand storm that is pyramidal monument. Its brick (flawed atom) and mortar (intangible rationality) fabric of actuality can be known from hints of text in that weft. (the intent of track is in reading) It may not be so easy to find and use a formula that invents itself in process as it assembles in and from a great equilibrium desert storm.

What genesis can focus unrestricted possibility into a miniscule phenomenal corridor? Existence does, and by fact of being observed, and knowing it, transcends itself. But of course, that must be realized. A crossing of sort may be suddenly or methodically made in any moment through a seeing instrument, (ibal) that possession as self is necessarily a part of. That must be location and in that new-age-double talk journey of citizen it may be referred to as a "time treasure." (egg may drop or be manipulated)

Where is harbinger of soul potential? Where is possibility of soul? It must be, as with all possibility, within Dark chaos maelstrom. If filament is caused to arrive in guise of a serpent and becomes entangled with other serpents perhaps the "gift" of such a collective energetic intertwining will create a quality of experience that enriches and embellishes contribution and hence essential positive property. It happened ages ago before history in a time ruled by serpents and was a great beginning. There may even still be equity in that.

Perhaps the Fifth will be a return of sorts to a situation of more soul awareness and interaction and less fear. That fragile thread is so important and that is "known," yet there may be a misinterpretation that results in extreme protection. That may be a false understanding. It may hurt when soul is bruised but that and the even much more extremes of possession are positive enhancement. Any "action" that may be shared or witnessed that involve soul are valid and positive. (be it subjectively,…..good or bad)

Results go far into beautitudes and beyond, past gate or dock and into quality of chaos reservoir. This is ultimate direction.

Provision for a potentially colossal deployment of a volume of resources not previously considered or even capable of consideration may be in the innocent befriending of a conceptual entity of unspecified opportunity. An almost casual rendering of intent involving a divine acquaintance.

* In dynamic of a soul filament nuance and rational organic star dust propagation of event contribution, selection must choose a meaningful sequence. Equilibrium will not give it rise and Holy trinity of perpetuity principle will be held accountable. It is with directive of "purpose," …… and if achieved will support a harbor of commerce, (as brief as will occur,) in order to embellish quality of energetic contribution, a trade of experience for virtue, grace or worth, or the Fifth of nine traditional

orders of hierarchy of angelic. It may be power of efficacy within citizen to thus accomplish.

Quotes from Skaay and Ghandl, poets of ancestral Haida clans.

"A secret that is in Fifth basket and the Fifth civilization is
that tide-walkers will fly."
"Reach through five baskets and in moment of the Fifth
interval Voicehandler (the singer) will give tide-
walkers their wings."

If ability to produce desired result can become common in the Fifth it will still not be a walk in the park and will come with a necessity to stretch arm and fingers of rationality in order to reach and release a secret of Fifth basket.

Citizen must hold and pursue in a possibly hostile energetic environment where anything and everything is comfort, while nothing,.... may quickly become quite uncomfortable.

Approaching the membrane invites a white noise chaos of that extreme pressure where a cognitive map will become blank. Dneipo encountered it in great Sea Mother's mouth at the bottom of the Indian Ocean and Vani took his small entourages into it as his wave tunnel erased "self" on the Pacific shore. Yet citizen must at this point continue starring at a non-window as fragility of being quivers in a meager bubble-cavern that barely shelters that which is rational from that which is not.

This is not circumstance and is pre-discerning and cannot be understood in pre-possession. It is same as when Dasein has nothing more outstanding,..... though temporary. (many tribes call it "little death")

There is a true unfragmented wholeness that ignores "moment" and no longer allows incompleteness of standing before self. In non-being heart beats quickly become wider and wider, but in purity of "care, desire, and will," creation, perhaps teaching and maybe even loving will recover recognizable being and citizen may continue into a subtle understanding. It sounds, and is quite sketchy at best, because it is far from contemporary status quo. (as are those tribal "coming of age" rituals)

Esoteric philosophies may help to balance movement through stages of that understanding. Though seamless the "condition" may beg measurement.

At historical primes, they have been represented by untold symbols and scribbles and in medieval times they have been represented by seven symbols of alchemy, the hieroglyphic monad. This caricature basically represents seven virtues,....wisdom, justice, temperance, fortitude, faith, hope and love.

An archetypal unity takes three stages to descend into complexity, wears the garment and retaining essence ascends via three stages of creative imagination to "Anthropus." He/she now begins to display as a rational organic exhibiting divine understanding.

"Passion" is a term that is used in describing that which is born of volatile primal energy. It will involve soul that becomes evident in lower vehicle. It may subjectively occur as good or evil and will always incur judgement.

Striding forth from a position of unbound grace and into a common familiar will invite doubt, question or even perhaps aggression. (Bruno)

A witness, community or civilization may be in such a previous absolute belief that a display of "passion" may become an attack on that belief. It has/is/and will be all to evident. It may be hope of an understanding of the Fifth that with patience of a Pythagorean class 101 "passion" may become regarded as "normal."

Is there a kettle containing all ingredients of a cosmic brine, and the last sprinkling of seasoning has been added? What would such a recipe require in order to simmer forth a broth of exquisite nourishment for an emaciated civilization?

Soul stitch of a delicate surgery is evidence of rationality within animal. Arrival of opposed thumbs helped in providing vehicle. It is presence of Dark chaos within light spectrum. It is awareness of self in consciousness. It is filament serpent entangled within organic with purpose of contribution. Infusion of energy that brought forth "experience" will be payed back with interest. Beautitude and hence Dark reservoir will receive embellishment.

Ibn¢ Arabi allots three degrees of prayer,
Presence/Audition/Vision

A student citizen of the Fifth will, with acceptance of responsibility and determination, hold volition against white noise, current and turbulence of chaos storm. They must first shelter in bubble-harbor that protects rational fragility even while it is exponentially inflated. They are in prayer of "audition." Creative imagination is strong and method of display is developing and maturing very quickly.

As that "passionate norm" becomes more thoroughly simmered and assimilated into witness, community or civilization a position of grace may be slowly revealed to those that are still in prayer of "presence."

Contribution may or may not be visible to this prayer. It may be considered an introduction to an elegant imaginative idea. Capacity may decide that involvement.

It most assuredly will be recognized by those that are with prayer of "vision." These are citizens who will now be carefully venturing outside of harbor and occasionally feeling absolute power of creation vortex.

In purity of "care, desire, will and confidence" creation, teaching, and perhaps loving will forward into subtle understanding, to "tune" the visionary to a radiant temperament.

The good fight of house of best purpose is fought in "audition prayer" and displayed in "vision prayer." "Owing presence" will and must forward yet it is absolute basic experience.

The Fifth civilization of human-kind will strive for "shared" spiritual enlightenment across game board (of Vani and Ron) and will come back from personal awareness to subtle introductions that they will understand as hints of direction for those in "prayer of presence."

* Power of audition has ability to soar into and remain in a spiritual. It is disturbing and extremely exciting. Yet ascension is only part of process, a return carries directive of suggestion. The bird soaring through top branches of creation tree cannot remain in that fascinating wonderland and an implication will be to come to ground.

Insight of higher realm will be carried into etheric body via exercise of a rhythmic "working moment." Essence can and will be woven into identity, possession and personal firmament.

In vim and vigor of situation may become, as in alchemy, point of "fixing the volatile." In a medieval search for enlightenment, (philosopher's stone) was the isolation of mercury from solution to form primal elixir by removing extremely foreign and poisonous elements. It was called "crucifying the serpent" (hmm wonder why?) and was ritual moving toward bridge of Horus Kings. It was identifying soul within rationality and utilizing rational soul to do so.

As in mercurial suggestion it may imaginatively present as soul filament serpents draped around and entwined with rationality cross. It was on the ancient staff or Caduceus of Hermes, was medieval sign of Magik and to this day is a sign of medical care.

In the fable of "Parzival" this "holiest" may be a sort of bowl arriving in organic splender from divinity. (perhaps not unlike the bowl on who's rim Vani and KiiJay stood at the birth of Carpadia) It will always be within vision of alchemists, sorcerers, wizards and shamans.

It is appropriate description for a vessel designed to hold divinity and being continually immersed in divinity, will indeed hold divinity. (a vessel designed to hold water and immersed in water will probably hold water)

Vessel is of course held in "possession" that is recognizable rational soul. An identity of fractal extrapolation of Dark chaos storm within,..... designed to "know" that presence and co-incidentally believe that all other "ones" also possess it.

Saint Symeon: "One who has become many remains the one undivided." All "ones" will contribute be they alien or familiar and that is purpose and so unimaginably diverse that "familiar" cannot even go there in imagination. It also pretty much guarantees continual contribution.

It does not involve a period of "time" but involves billions of "periods of time." This might be display of where-ever and when-ever and indeed is "some-where over the rainbow."

As in physics, ultimate uncertainty principle declares that position and momentum (direction) of one of the ones cannot be determined at the same time. There might be a same although probably only similar location and goal (except for contribution) available at any one of extreme multitude of work moments in Dark ever-near.

Perhaps valuable that citizen may be able to sort through weft to filter essence from identity and possession, though weaving is initially without seam. In prayer of "audition" is labor of work moment. Presence and vision are of necessity basically ignorant of struggle.

How many, where, in what creative imagination and by which method will they move into "audition." With a guide?

Exponentially inflated creative imagination is strong and methods of display may be tempered with a reminder of "brother/sisterhood." Homeric Path is littered with heart-organs that were used to bring desire into manifestation and each marker was most certainly not as simple as hatching intent like an emerald/blue bird. Each "one" of the brother/sisterhood struggled through "audition" prayer and some were mentored in, while others pleaded with their presence prayer for blessing and yet others were able to stand on the shoulders of great citizens who had gone before, just to be able to peer a little farther.

Many trials/trails and adjustments to creation path may have occasionally received advise from a guide or mentor and droppings of Divine concepts may have helped point the way, yet there would still have been a significant amount of "wandering." (how long were the tribes of Israel wandering in a desert?) Every citizen of "the way" will, past, present, or future recognize it as invasion by a trivial mundane or social media machine. This seepage must be counteracted with focus and attention perhaps as a cautionary withdrawal from busyness. Any leak must be from heart, not into it. From soul, not into it.

In work moment audition of arts, music or any creation idea citizen must be judge of virtue, truth and grace. Left to a yoke fitted populace of presence prayer, disappointment and doubt may seep into soul.

Spiritual maturity will begin to relax into an acceptance of pure, cold, Dark, unbridled chaos of non-being to draw inspiration from a non-limiting reservoir. If serpent filament of soul allows "that" leak into rationality the better for all concerned. (intents and purposes)

If origin of creation act is submerged in that reservoir then the "stuff" of that supply must be in creation. One might see that glorious arrival if they have become visionary prayer "tuned" to such a radiant temperament.

From ancient Hindu awareness:…."This is wisdom one cannot learn, they must become it." It is sustaining a vulnerable position where an invited power of transformation may act upon a willing citizen in countenance of little or no clutter or clamor. An almost suspended calm sanctuary of that turbulent well of souls is still a place of great trust. A dreamer would do well to find, hold and become "care" of that house of best purpose.

This is a wisdom of "intentional position" with a largely reduced complexity because it is "out on a limb."

"adaptation of poem by Rumi"

A trembling leaf seems to dance in wind.
It is also the dance of "ones."
Continuous in joy of light
Is "hiding" Dark divinity.

A visionary should never fear being alone in mortality, for it is the secret condition of hero/heroin and one among faces of God.

Floating higher in the vault than a universe allows perspective of a greatly reduced cosmos. Creation worlds are not linear but "thick" and simply await "touch" of soul.

Dark essence is beyond and transcends all being but energy of that source may appear as action of becoming. Be it heavenly lightning bolt, radiant angel or atomic bomb an act of existing is not divinity but in familiar realm of experience. Dark is still hidden silence while vitality of it is heard and seen in spectrum, revealed by soul of intent.

143

It is an abstract reservoir that can never be personally experienced and "believing" that is "freedom within light."

It may be about a "peace" that is obtained within frequency of light and in almost casually pursuing heart's desire with a sublime elegance of soul bearing a Dark mysterious.

Citizen will not be found in a frantic state, scrambling for ideas of their fulfilment, yet they may often be recognized in some form of its pursuit. Focus, attention and balance may lead to a long and rich contribution. It is actually quite observable when encountered (not often enough) in a relaxation within vision prayer and a continued dabbling in audition prayer. Visionaries almost always feel a need to dabble.

Familiar manifest as a reflection of intent of pure soul is appropriately,....perfect. Dark, divine energy may be potential fuel of an unapproachable combustion that with spark brings (gravity) rent in heavenly capacity (location) to forward "point heat" and eventual work moment experience, which is contribution and purpose.

One can never speak of being immersed in reservoir but perhaps occasionally a ladle may be brought to lips. If not a ladle then possibly a sip and if not a sip then hopefully a thirst for the nutrient vitality of that cool, deep, Dark well of potentiality. In an enduring simplicity direction of some creative citizens of the Fifth may be to reveal that thirst. All manner of unveiling will present and it is responsibility of citizen to self-monitor virtue, truth and grace of their contribution.

Indeed, within prayer of audition, they must know how to construct house of best purpose before a practitioner of prayer of presence encounters it.

A student-citizen accepts a great responsibility and yet carries it with a lightness of heart. Hence there should be no rushing through work moment. One might not run toward a sunrise but let it wash over themselves. Its occurrence is perfect and then it has "happened." Has contribution been a slow, rich quality of expression or a haphazard, worried and hurried wandering through a wilderness?

Baal Shem Tov of ancient Polish Jewish legend believed that, "to live is to serve God." Sounds like contribution of experience to augment

Dark chaos sea. Existence may be simple decisions and choices under that certainty. The simple will endure.

So it is into the Fifth with confidence of a redeeming savior- child. Good/bad, plus/minus, positive/negative character of creation from a point of view beyond a universe is non-issue. Be it, and so be it pleasure or pain opportunity of creative awareness is issue. Quite often an "awakening" will arrive from a very negative experience.

From one of subjectively most despicable rational situations, that of imprisonment, will sometime develop a member of the Fifth who has/ will use isolation to forward great contribution. That may be a special circumstance but it would not be detrimental for any student-citizen to remove themselves from busyness and frivolity. Some may dedicate the first part of their life to social, travel and/or career foraging and then later relax into headier pursuits of temperament of the Fifth. If this is a conscious decision made while quite young all the more power, for variety of experience and novelty of alternative adventure will allow great contribution on many fronts.

In fact, a yogi-sage who hides himself away in complete seclusion may indeed create a great masterpiece. It is huge contribution and well recognized and yet it may seem like a very large price to pay. Perhaps better to enter into such an intense work-moment dedication after simply enjoying a few hundred thousand of the more trivial. "All" experience will contribute.

It may also be suggested that a situation of adult adolescence and lost purpose in old growth could result in a numbing, kind of "vacant" unpleasantness. How wonderful to be blessed with direction, realized contribution and feeling of embellishment administered,..... right up until the light frequency goes out. Dark will receive that gift as long as it will be given.

Each moment of that supplement and the k-zillions of others help fortify oozing, spitting, roiling and boiling Dark chaos sea of possibility that will blend contribution from unlimited, unimaginable and impossibly foreign donors.

Is there a kettle containing all possible energy ingredients in a brine of all possible cosmic spheres? Has even the last few moments been sprinkled as seasoning to instill deepest flavor? What more could this recipe require in order to simmer forth a broth of the most exquisite nourishment for introduction of a new point creation - nuclear furnace - rational organic - civilization.

This is return, but completely different, process of a creation realm that will forward throughout many ages and wait patiently. (as "time" will not exist) "Sooner or later" or perhaps not, a vessel that is capable of holding divinity while immersed in divinity and of creating "time" from homeostatic irritant, will evolve and in that presentation request rationality as method of recognizing experience. That energy loan will be forthwith granted and for thousands of generations and perhaps with luck even eras, payback contribution will continue until the last moment of supplement. Dark will receive as long as will be given.

That broth as a continually embellished source may be soup of a truly unlimited creation opportunity. It could and probably does exist far, far beyond the most extreme limit that "familiar" rational organic might be able to imagine. Almost as if light spectrum was/is limit of imagination.

Yet citizen must use all innuendos of allegory, spirit, relativity, science, symbolism and of course grace to grasp at serpent filament soul strings of that which will allow creation.

This must be Magik speaking,....

describing Dark energy that was not born and will not die. Associated for a "time" with rational organic with an intention of embellishment. A soul filament extrapolated from reservoir of chaos-soul and displayed in limited belief of self-realization. Source being inconceivable and uncreated. Moment being created and "in attendance."

Can and should a citizen/student fall into enchantment? Not enthusiasm but something more of an inexplicable conjuring of probable imaginative? Why was transcendental always more easily embraced than immanent?

It may be a "method" of directive in "pushing" into that which has not been described, is not registered, is not held in presence prayer and has not been confirmed.

Dark is not "above," or "out there" nor even "within" citizen but encompassing, separate and yet a part of. Reciprocal relation of Dark soul and rationality is still an act of revealing, as action and experience and manifest unisphere carries extreme fertility as blessing from. Ultimate chaos contains all possibility, including light frequency and quite probably only "living in that freedom" reveals the idea of Dark. Once realized creation becomes fulfilment.

Again, as Hildegard of Bingen described Dark, "I stir everything into quickness with a certain invisibility which sustains all. I am the fiery power, yet my essence lies hidden in these things as they blaze from me." Personified, yes, but still an ancient citizen of the Fifth. Hildegard had fallen into enchantment.

Subtleness of occurrence should not necessarily be as easy as the analogy of a fragile web drifting on a stormy wind-swept tempest until barely hooking onto a shaky leaf-like island. Rational organic is an even more critically balanced tight rope walker as they scurry along an ever increasing "quickness" uphill in rain. Even a slightest puff of chaos wind from an acute angle could bring demise.

The great "Nuendo" could not take his attention off of narrow path on which he balanced and neither can rational focus on that miniscule reflection they see toying from their peripheral. If that is oblivion and his attention goes to it result may be a catastrophe.

No, rope walker, like tide walker must with one foot after another make extreme haste. They must "get ahead, acquire, accumulate, and propagate."

Of course, if either "one" embraced that which oblivion was trying to point out, they might discover the wings that were tightly folded across their backs. (even Vanisila and Carpadia wore theirs for years without discovery) (the shaman of San peoples included wings as absolute security in ecstatic adventure) (the N.W. Haida told of "sapsucker" who would bring tide- walkers to their wings) In all cases that would pretty much negate worry of balance, narrowness and precariousness of a thin line stretching out into possibility fog.

Wings are appendage of choice for citizen of the Fifth. They are redemption across expanse of "oneness." They honor savior-child by displaying divinity also within saved. They are "method" of the angelic and indeed,...... open another dimension. It is easier to understand soul if one can reach a vault of souls. All of the Carpatian disciples had access to this vault and those lofty abilities helped them prepare for the meeting at Holoflux at a "darwish" of the Fifth and on the Fifth anniversary of Carpadia's arrival. A great sky-light was opened and any potential student-citizen need no longer climb or be hauled up.

Adapted from "The Alchemical wedding of Christian Rosenkreutz:

"The adepts can only ascend by using one of three instruments. Those with "wings" can immediately project to a spiritual awareness and this corresponds to visionary citizen. Those with "ladders" strive to build a link in their souls between the mundane and spirit knowledge and then to confidently climb. (audition) Those with "rope" need assistance from above, perhaps a mentor. When convinced, they realize a personal "will" to pull against commonplace. (presence)"

Does living in freedom of light with wings on ones back reveal Dark which allows realization of said wings?

Subtleness of occurrence may even be sketchier then that.

How about a critically balanced blindfolded tight rope walker scurrying, (because there is a time limit) along an exponentially increasing "quickness" uphill in a raging blizzard while on a fractally fragile web, drifting on a stormy, chaotic, windswept tempest until barely and by sheer chance hooking onto a trembling leaf-like island that jiggles and squiggles and occasionally spews fire or inundates presence with far too copious amounts of wind and water?

Yet as fun as that was it does not do justice to the odds of circumstance coming into a fruit bearing situation. Opportunity is with every one of the ones for contribution and every one will contribute. That is fundamental.

One might suppose that, as in a question of wings and freedom it would be freedom that unveiled wings. Living freely within light does not mean tripping out in hippie-land, but it does mean becoming aware of how and why the condition and situation of rational organic has come to be. That circumstance is not a "great mystery" or "in the hands of a God." (not as a personification) A great mysterious God realm is simply

Dark chaos reservoir of possibility. Equally inaccessible true, yet Dark can, within disciplines of spirit, physics, philosophy, mathematics or any other pursuable art or passion become visible to the heart,..... as it is in filamentary representation,......soul.

As a Chaos God,.....Dark contains absolute grace and absolute evil and any manifestation that rational imagination may forward is a pale fragment of the totality. It is so do to extreme limits imposed upon rational situation and that is the "reason" of it.

A visionary citizen will understand the transformation and permanence of energy. Rational experience creates contribution returned to investment opportunity reservoir as energy.

A possibility forum was brought into the material and was recognized as action. It acknowledged identity and contribution according to capacity. When organic systems could no longer support self, contribution was ended yet even that minute embellishment was held in Dark forever and available in various combinations with donations of other "ones" for re-investment. It is for rational organic and all other contributors' salvation from oblivion, "in energy essence only." No part, parcel or portion of identity will go with.

From cold Dark chaos into photon spark of light energy frequencies and back into slightly embellished cold Dark chaos. "One" simple energy oscillation.

A true visionary sage of the Fifth may have to hold soul filament of heart up before mirror-lens-window of material manifest in order to illuminate true intent from shadow of image. It is a bold prayer that can only result in complete creative fulfilment as "one" lives open and aware of freedom within light.

If/when this dream occurs, after audition and well into vision prayer, it will "happen" just within tenacious membrane of actuality and will be as fragile as divinity of that activation. The walk of a sage is then along a razor's edge of shifting sea of desert dunes. Haunting music of a great scirocco swirls fantastic foreign frequencies right up to but not into heart and soul. Presences murmur and glance past peripherally in a total wilderness just at edge of rational organic vitality and path is continually changing. Being may be granted a type of "foresight" with imagination but that does not necessarily make it so. It will be an unveiled "intent" of heart's desire that will descend Sufi-mystic "hadras" of possibility,…. to become.

A citizen within 'vision" prayer is one grain of sand in a vast chaos desert and knows it. Nodules of such a critical walk begin to converge at hour-glass restriction as "time" itself becomes cinched in at this moment-narrows of awareness. Each adept, be they in familiar or foreign cosmos may then briefly glance to the side, into that oblivion and in that omnipotent blink a great vast Dark storm will reflect back true essence of each precious contributory crystal. (before continuing into the next abundance)

Significant opportunity may affect border and membrane limiting occurrence and may be a provision for recognition of a volume of frequency resource not previously considered or even capable of consideration.

A great bell of creative intention has just been intoned.

The "narrowing" will bring true blessedness out from prayer of presence and into audition and those in audition may move to prayer of vision. A presentation of increasing novel criteria and a push into diverse frequencies may illuminate the idea of a visionary civilization.

The Fifth Civilization of Rational Organic

This is the edge of dream. Recognition not only of "what" is being acknowledged but "that" it is being acknowledged. A citizen is holding volition and willing heart's desire as divine answer to that which is being inquired after. It is soul affirming the presence of soul creation.

Fragility of such an occasion is important as that will result in a fragile civilization, but far better to forward this moody creative sensitivity of water-bearer than that of a hard line, selfish civilian of the Fourth.

The Fifth would do well to put house of best purpose on display for it may be approaching a "time" when it might be noticed.

Of course, recognizing a rationality that binds together so many linear forces and qualities can be very confusing within the debris by which it is defined. Thus, there is suggestion of a certain withdrawal into a sticky, wet, capricious sincerity deep in soul-well. Perhaps a place where the clock does not tick-tock quite so loud, where not Chronos God of "time" rules but Kairos God of "timing."

In chronological civilizations civilians move into the future but in kairological civilizations time rolls over residents. Some of the most creative and imaginative citizens of the Fifth lived in ancient kairological timing. It was "once upon a time" in a "happily ever after."

In heat of one's passion and awareness and in whatever situation, phenomenal or spiritual, when presented, a next step must be taken. It will never be offered with an expectation of refusal. Adapted from Quaballah; "Divinity will be made visible by this type of work, this is Elohim's presence in creation."

Working with Divine consent and assistance requires being visible. Energy whirlwind is invisible but in presence of water it is defined by water, in presence of sand is defined by sand and in presence of rationality is defined by debris of material qualities. Yet that non-local vortex may blow straight through a rational mind-socket with little resistance, as manifestation, from a point of view beyond a universe is quite inconsequential.

A visionary citizen might have to cover themselves with runes and hieroglyphs and spray themselves with "dragon spam" just that they might get recognized.

The pilgrim caricature of the Fifth must in some way fold that tornado into corners and quoins to stabilize it and suggest "knowing" it but that is while riding on the back of a serpent traversing the ever-changing desert dunes while a scirocco blows its strongest.

Working with Divine consent and assistance requires being immersed in the passion of heart's desire. That will present in all realms and when this type of work is made visible Dark God will bless it with "encouragement."

In the Fifth, membranes are indeed thinner between lookout and pilgrim, soul and shadow, untouchable and dance and foreign and familiar. The "spark" of Jesus is just over there. Adaptation of Hildigard of Bingen describing Dark divinity; "I am the fiery power, yet my essence lies hidden in thee as thou blazeth from me." Two of simple criteria for primal point-rent might be safe haven from ultimate tempest and organic tinder.

Citizen adept will welcome blessing but also realize the proximity of a fiery core of chaos energy, only a meniscus (caused by surface tension) away from their personal and that of their civilization's quite necessary,....... order.

Path is intended to bring tide-walkers to their wings and so it just makes sense that it is not a stroll in the park. Those in vision and audition prayers must create a full dream before those in presence prayer are exposed to it. Hysteria, confusion and danger of simply unveiling such a gift would at least begin to break down order and at worst turn a now angry mob upon those enlightened ones who would share.

Examples abound throughout ages but the one that keeps coming around is that of Giordano Bruno. As the most famous self-declared heretic of the Inquisition he said things like, "most things are not only made by God but are made of God." Commonplace tide walkers of presence prayer in his day,.....burned him at the stake. (though he was correct)

When Dark divine influence becomes visible as soul filaments of heart attained vision becomes receptacle of worshipper's being "in measure of its capacity." It may be wise and there may be a built-in safeguard to the overloading of that receptacle. The catch may be a simple trait of most rationals and that is mistrust and suspicion of novelty or difference. It usually leads to an innocent turning of eye, with no real damage or gain. (but of course that is fundamental of gain)

That is why "personal responsibility" and "attention" hold such significant posture in entering audition prayer. These are attributes that successfully cut away chaff of simply owing presence. From there the Castalian code may be advantageous. "Attain utmost command of one's passion and keep self and passion vital and flexible by forever recognizing its ties with all other passionate disciplines."

One is on a way toward enhanced contribution of self, perhaps leading to great contribution. One may now become involved in creative design. One begins to feel fulfilment of contribution which immediately suggests correct direction. (though a lot of wandering may still occur)

When creative intention inundates, "measure of capacity" is augmented and receptacle of worshipper's being becomes full of soul.

That is access to chaos cauldron of all possibility and not hypothetically. If soul is fractal extrapolation of Dark chaos reservoir then that filament is a miniscule representation of the whole, not a portion of it.

This is supply of trust and surrender, it is personal responsibility and attention of self and soul. It may be release, unveiling and freedom within light yet always, in a corner of every moment,...... is Dark presence.

Imagination may want to suggest a move in concept beyond spectral frequencies and toward an occult imagery of possibility. "Action" of it is futile so perhaps one must approach from the back of "Michipeshu." In such a fiercely docile posture, as the omnipotent serpent soars over ocean, lake, mountain and desert, chaos wind will blow hard. One does not let go at this "moment."

It may be when the Fifth river approaches that serpents are carried forward with current and a divine contrivance. Soul filaments that entwine in sweet song, contrast familiar frequency oscillations, watch their shadows break away to be again with Dark, hear strange and ancient echoes that rush up to their hearts but do not enter and still, they sit quietly in their canoes.

Because they are at an "immovable place," "world navel" and Holoflux "yowa." A place where divinity arrives or rationality departs. There is pure confidence at that "gate," where a hinged or pivoting guardian clicks at the "pawl" that regulates access or departure and monitors limit and extreme abundance. It is a "timely" device of rational imagination within citizen, balancing God energy and hero/heroin identity.

On the back of a great serpent one is careful not to let go and to peer cautiously into a biting wind that will tear flesh to feed creation. Perhaps a daunting task for commonplace so a sustainable unique enthusiasm must prevail. At this darwish dream makers weave corporality into weft with half magik and half star dust. Then intention falls into rapture as vivification displays fulfilment of first cause. This is "moment-bead" of creation and "is" immovable navel of being,.….it has "happened." It is no longer motion.

Occurrence is precious as contribution of rationality and that presence if accentuated by great abundance of possibility that the Fifth will open, forwards an exponentially enhancing quality. Dark reservoir becomes "thicker" and other creations are therefore more rich,.….and so on.

Simplicity endures and this may be the simplest "method" of purpose. It will eventually involve a significant complexity to arrive at such a humble, unique, sustainable enthusiasm.

Claire and Dneipo found this stillness after an invisible vortex scattered their rational debris to the cardinals. Each disciple learned where to find it and each citizen will know this center. A civilization that understands its own navel should be happy to display it across a familiar cosmos. (everything within light spectrum cosmos is familiar)

It is a tiny harbor and in all probability will be completely unnoticed, yet why not present from house of best purpose. Embellishing Dark God is best purpose as each moment contribution is first cause and therefore "encouraged" by Dark. (though miniscule it is still a drop in a big bucket)

What of Dark taking its place in corner of every moment? Socrates: "know thyself." Not so radical, as origin of creation was from the Divine, so divinity must be within rational organic. It brought ability to worship and is almost "cheesy" in its cornpone idea of suggestion. (God instilling soul in man in order to worship God) (valid but for personification)

Yet that, was only an ancient belief. In order to get "presence prayer" to comprehend, it must have been done by personification. An idea developed independently in civilizations globally who had no apparent contact. Of course they did, but not on a planetary rind. Personifying deities was an evolutionary action of all rationality taking place at that "time" but not simultaneously,…. in "audition" or "vision" prayers. They created the Dream that others would follow. They emerged when Kairos, God of "timing" was auspicious. Some have gone and others have lasted a few thousand years but they are rapidly fading. Not really that enduring.

Dark in every corner of every moment of every contribution is simplicity of endurance. True examples are always of the same suggestion. This is truth and grace of chaos possibility.

Welcome the Fifth Civilization of Rational Organic.

Perhaps this is a situation when hero/heroin is not afraid to be seen with or without clothes. Seriously, put a priest or Imam in front of a group of practitioners in genes and a t-shirt. Watch the exit door spin. That is sad because at end of the Fourth any hocus-pocus (as in ego house of cards) should be over with.

General populace should have a better understanding but many distractions arrive so rapidly. These distractions are the engine of consumerism and are indeed a global infestation.

The Fifth is thorough and complete. Accepting membership into the Fifth cannot be undone. A citizen adept now knows a truth that they cannot ever forget. To take one's leisure within the light of creation while knowing Dark encouragement is a true sincerity of "knowing thyself." It is ultimately private but never lonely. When star-dust condenses into self-realization path of solitude is defined and complete "sharing" without identity will not occur until star-dust releases energy within its matter to contribute even that to necessary Dark reservoir.

Self-awareness of rational organic citizen of the Fifth is cognizant of in and how rational organics occur. Not simply within manifest complexity nor struggling upon the rind of planetary consciousness, but in soul-pulpy, spiritually spongy and unispherically attuned recipients of the message and implication of Dark Salt/Dark Soul.

Reason in rationality forwards purpose in divinity. Action of Holy Trinity as investment is indifferent to divine and rational or God and organic.

It is the simplest "method" of obtaining goal of Dark realm, a pattern disengaged from design by autonomy, yet still a very elegant suggestive hint.

Citizen poet writes;	"In a cave Magik sits before the fire that can only be lit more than one time in one place He is patiently anxious to again bring star powder of one hand into relationship With Dark energy of the other.
Citizen musician plays;	"the song of a swinging gate whose squeaking hinge recognizes and describes creative process and sings about "purpose."
Citizen artist paints;	"the emerald green aura of every "Hadra" and "Sephiroth" between the manifest and divinity and illustrates differentiation and assimilation according to each necessary expression."
Citizen shaman;	"understands the potential inhabitants of the "Fifth Basket." He may "conjure up" and/or help incubate those "potencies."
Citizen dreamer;	"floats higher than a universe and even higher than a vault of souls. Each is participatory in various levels of creation and thus unfinished. The true ingredient of a dream must be imagination."

Can one imagine being almost completely insignificant? Can one imagine being reduced to simple rational energy donation? Station and success will be qualitative with appropriate recognition and that is embellishment, yet ego as activator may be sub-rational nemesis of purpose contribution.

So,….where is the citizen? Rationality is necessary for contribution. A "qualitative," creating embellishment is thicker than owing presence. Being part of beginning a dream as a Voicehandler, sings the song that approaches harmony of the Fifth. They lean toward position of acknowledged citizen visionary. They lean toward purpose.

The bull-rational of either gender in owing presence might somehow know that it is stud. Ego of it is animal. It will result in minimal maintenance contribution. Dream ingredient may actually be a variable of possibility in influential access and manifestation.

Citizen may venture, not into but very near interval. (just before entering a star, "Stormbringer" pulled into a small sanctuary, "Ttsaa'ahl")

(the event horizon of a black hole)

Peripheral qualities in such situations must get noticed quickly and focused upon and these distractions would hopefully persist and increase. One might trust them. It was recognized psycho-sociologically in,…."A beautiful mind, the life of John Nash." Within cosmos or within mind, once initiated they will not go away (accepting membership cannot be undone) but one must look at and through them in order to augment appropriately. Sitting on the event horizon of a Dark singularity watching "time" disappear might present one with a fairly "heavy" experiential contribution.

Citizens may and should feel like they are riding on the back of a great serpent as it traverses the razor edge of shifting dunes through a chaos desert of possibility.

Citizens may and should feel a simplicity of rational energy donation. One of miniscule ones in an eternal energy supplement beyond cosmos that still results in salvation from oblivion. (without identity)

It may again be very simple, ….supporting purpose with reward.

There is a truth and grace in Dark chaos. As was emphasized in Christian scripture, "Satan is in the material while God is not, "and,…. by the way,….. any entire universal cosmos is material. The only extension into manifestation that pristine Dark has is soul filament. It allows rationality that allows contribution and as such embellishment of chaos reservoir.

(God instilling soul in man in order to worship God) At end of "life" Satan can have the body while God retains soul. That may be an artistic truism.

Dark chaos never "gets back" soul filament because it was always in possession, as a fractal extrapolation of Dark chaos. Soul was/is the Magik of all creations. It would be "absolutely necessary" in any alternative form of contribution whenever and wherever. In a certain realization "that" should be quite comforting to familiar rational organic.

No matter what size, shape, material, function, or positioning of a completely foreign "contributor," they will have soul and in that way, be within "family" of the created.

When motion of moment has passed it is no longer action but has "happened." Contribution was made and that occurrence may now have an immovable place. Some may say that it remains forever in History, yet that acknowledgement can only survive if History survives. That will not "happen."

If previous motion is only maintained in motion then occurrence cannot hold an immovable place. The "happening" is just one of the ones.

(peace out baby) Only moment brevity has position.

Act of "being" seems to be getting simpler all the "time."

Responsibility may be with citizen. They are rationally accountable for awareness of how and why rational organics occur.

Creating awareness of dream is probably an unveiling of imaginative moment while in audition prayer. It may arrive from persistent, peripheral distraction and that is not status quo.

Novelty would not be the work of Satan and even when one hears voices or sees visions a suggestion will usually be of their divine nature. It is evident how enthusiastic all religious faiths were about novel ecstatic vision. Birthing idea of Gods from peripheral distraction of norm might suggest that citizen should pay attention to any especially persistent dream ingredient, as it may be conclusive variable of possibility in access, ability and with determination,…..manifest content.

Once initiated they will not go away. One must look at and through them in order to contribute a rich, thick, soul-pulpy grace to a reservoir of rich, thick, soul-pulpy grace. (membership cannot be undone)

Dark Salt, …"pre-cosmological incidence of Dark matter coming out of solution/solution of Dark energy and providing crystalline form to become irritant, that with gravitational "pressure" will rupture membrane of cosmic background radiation to form point creation, hence nuclear furnace and then rational organic."

Dark Soul,… "fractal extrapolation of Dark thread like soul filament snaking its way into heart organ of appropriate organic recipient to bring recognition of self as a rational and open a long awaited gate of worship and contribution."

Will citizen adept move into distractions as John Nash may have finally managed or tumble around the edge of a galaxy in the manner of George Cantor? Some choices are relatively easy yet others may require,……patience. In imprisonment of a medieval tower contribution may have been easier than in any and all modern cities and cultures.

A citizen may initiate something that will not go away. It is not modern, nor is it ancient, yet in whatever vital and flexible creative discipline that may be its becoming, within the Fifth, there must be an almost imperative suggestion of house of best purpose.

Recognition may be forth-with yet citizen might come into dream knowledge with script already prepared from sages locked in medieval towers. The ones that realized their perfect opportunity did not raise their banner but worked uninterrupted. They used their wings to fly above their cell to the next. Some may have used ladders to climb with their understanding to the next and perhaps others were dropped a rope that they might climb into the Fifth.

Coming into dream, all prepared, is what many analysts said happened to ancient Egyptians. Their cosmological, natural and even social concepts were too "advanced" to have been learned the long way around by trial and error. (those ancients "paid attention")

Yet there will be untold numbers of adepts without banner. The "ones" diligent in gray but not quite yet in Dark. A citizen "muhip" must spin away phenomenal debris, recognize their flexible and vital passion and watch for the flag that is not of nation nor even of cosmos.

Vision prayer may be very necessary in order to raise those guiding principles. Causes and philosophies flap in the breeze of Tibetian prayer flags and tumble within Buddhist prayer wheels and there is of course so much more tumbling and flapping out there.

As they are everywhere the "muhip" may need to get never-where. A quiet immovable center sounds like the necessary eye of hurricane. If previous motion is only maintained by motion then occurrence cannot hold position,....ever, except,.....

Certainly not in a heaven or hell but quite possibly only within the brevity of moment itself. A suggestion has been offered of a prepared moment. Coming into a "prepared" dream does not seem valid. How would that happen? Is that "alien" interpretation of influence possible, though without all the drama? Do the ancestors really have dreams about pre-time?

Perhaps readiness of preplan is wrapped within soul filament and entangles throughout conscious organic to instill rationality and perhaps in circumstance of "able and willing" any foreign energy of chaos reservoir does in fact "prepare" one for contribution. (like an irritant wrapped in layers of time)

It is in thread that leads back through phenomenal labyrinth to gate. It is filament of Dark chaos that brings all rational organics back to reservoir of Dark chaos but while in rationality uninterruptedly declares aloud that "anything is possible." (this is not fundamentally of "order")

As result of blossoming technology and a spiritual openness that must accompany it, borders of rational organic have been pushed farther and farther into the previously unknowable. Wave function (information) of quantum particle cannot be precisely known (momentum and position, speed and location) because motion is only maintained by motion and quantum occurrence cannot ever "hold" for observation. It is in many potentialities until "collapsed" (limited) to one, "observable at moment brevity" and then energy of it is immediately returned to possibility. This system is dynamic.

A rational cannot obtain information about an unordered state though its function is introduced and maintained by an extrapolation of just such an imaginative "field reservoir." That maintenance parameter is minimum, it is "owing presence" and "presence prayer."

One might ask those of audition and vision prayers and fortify the advantage of going into medieval towers to create a great dream in house of best purpose and raise that banner high above the equilibrium horizon to suggest that though that simple maintenance restricts circumstance, it is still a variable.

This system is dynamic and although a path is set out a great deal of wandering is still available. It will be "citizen of the Fifth" who must accept rational accountability to challenge and push factors of awareness from presence into audition and finally into vision. Each citizen must contribute this communion as a civilization reflects upon its navel and moves past inherited legacy of animal and toward cosmic assembly of star-dust.

It almost seems like human existence has been "ashamed" of itself. As intent, heart's desire, motive, will and imagination usually help usher in manifestation, a quick look at the prior Four may seem to support that theory. With a meager sprinkling of a hand full of citizens of the Fifth those four eras have been very well known for their "contributions." All is contribution but perhaps it is better that technology has/will not advance to display and make known the "yowa" of humankind until after the Fifth civilization of humankind.

When that moment brevity is upon those who would display it, with an entire civilization in audition and vision prayers, there may come forward the answer by that which was inquired after.

At this, end of the Fourth, may be required a piety of concern. In that multitude of potentiality are those that hold a purity and grace and they must be immediately brought into dream in order to contribute. Those in audition must complete and present dream before presence is blinded by screen. (media) It is a bold prayer.

A need for quality contribution is greater than ever and responsibility for it now falls upon citizen adept. Forge icon, raise banner or display Dark beacon. Perhaps learn to navigate influence of Dark sea and in knowing and comprehending route of (God) encouragement, beautiful suggestions of direction may issue forth to become influential embellishment of non-identity in eternal energy realm,.... an extraordinary experience of aesthetics as donation of significant energetic supplement.

A rational cannot obtain information about an un-ordered state but can,.... in first cause,..... contribute to it.

Inherited animal legacy, or cosmic assembly of star dust, …it might be all the better for human-kind if the Fifth is able to firmly establish a civilization in house of best purpose. This is also a bold prayer.

At the end of Four, a pendulum seems to be swinging away from this necessary awareness yet it will and must repair to a much higher apogee.

(A description of situation is now available and that is first step on high road to salvation of rational organic.)

There will, in a distant work moment, occur discovery of a minute harbor of commerce that involves energy trade of a rationality with . divinity. It may be recognized by an alternative "system" that has learned to navigate influence of Dark sea. (God) Encouragement would certainly leave a "track" and that always holds eventual purpose of a "finding."

When that moment brevity is upon the civilization that would display it does it "intend" to be photographed as "just out of animal" or as a mature contributor towards beautitude and hence purpose,..… in form of cosmic assembly of star dust. (a human is wretched as animal and yet angelic in cosmology) Weaponize soul with grace, elegance, beauty and dignity of form.

It may seem like a very faraway place and time but that of course is now, in this moment brevity, just at the periphery of awareness, when in hour-glass narrows Dark allows reflection of soul. It is such a fantastic process as acknowledgement and is quite remarkable that "identity" may be capable of knowing its "situation."

An answer by that which was inquired after is, "an awakening to human condition by a system other than rational organic, and then communicated to rational organic."

When that occurs Horton, professor "Who" and the voices on a tiny dust speck on the professor's lap will open navigation in each of their unique "prendas" on a great, virgin Dark chaos maelstrom sea.

This sea was named Kalunga by the Bakongo people many generations prior. For spiritual awareness one must "sing and draw point." This is a visionary combination to mark contact between possessions of enlightenment,.. the vessels of which are prendas. These ritual vessels always contain cargo, tracings of the "yowa" of their familiar location or situation. (home) (adapted from "Hero with an African Face",...Clyde W. Ford)

Perhaps this may sound like, "a basic unit capable of forwarding familiar characteristics from one generation to the next." (a gene?)

Size and purpose of each prenda is exactly the same though participants may be from very different scales. This may be part of the frustration of rational organic. They perceive self as big, too big and yet are minute in a tiny harbor of energy commerce. The "scale" of participants would be most likely criteria of keeping them separated and unknown from each other.

These prendas may be vehicles of intercourse, the same in almost all forages or voyages into exchange of absolute/fundamental information regarding building block foundation of creative process. By objectivity they carry a sequence of "order" as it is encountered. "Locus" or fixed position of moment brevity of rational organic is forwarded to rational organic. If that can be accepted as mature contribution toward beautitude in form of cosmic assembly of star dust, then a civilization,.....

-first, would have to be well into the Fifth, just to recognize it
-second, would be in a good position to continue forwarding
    ideas of audition and vision prayers.
-third, would be unashamed to display and make known the
    "yowa "of humankind.

Setting out on "kalunga" in a ritual vessel may be relatively easy but finding a harbor, beach-head or pin head of commerce, entangled in overlapping perpendicular, vertically rotated stratum of energy weft may be more difficult. Where in that great birth canal potentiality will a search endeavor to locate Ttsaa'ahl?

Yet just before passing through a star and dispersing into Dark quantum, a Stormbringer prenda may encounter the fragile sanctity of a fertile cove. It is always there in nodal interlace of its burnt orange spectral frequency at gravity induced rent of point creation. The coercion causes a bursting forth with incredible speed and it begins to "de-couple." This is action of conceiving a universe. It is a changing from homogenous Dark energy sea into a clumpy cosmos, illustrating forms of complexity. Rationality is then "just down the road."

At this "one" single energy oscillation a rational, visionary citizen should "get it." Perhaps this situation has happened before, at other galaxian equatorial crossings. Maybe planned purpose of star cave is incremental positive adjustment of rational awareness, from presence and into audition and vision prayer to the Fifth.

This may be when all contribution can be knowable and eddies, whirlpools and currents of a raging turmoil of possibility may be intuited, juxtaposed or even mapped on charts. (though they are perpetually in chaotic motion of a continual morphology and change.) (a chart not easily read)

It may be perhaps similar to an "ibal" or seeing instrument, or perhaps similar to a "Popul Vuh." Symbolic alphabets will not be able to describe it. Nor will diagram nor video. It will not be able to be folded, bringing widely separated event circumstance into proximity. It is/will be "absolutely dynamic." A roiling indicator of Dark God encouragement. No moment brevity at this intimate distance. The situation may beg a certain "type" of talented interaction.

There are those who would be navigators.

They are well known for the extremely exotic emerald green aura in which they must reside. They must be saturated by it and in it and always remain there. They breath this aura and eat it, they can access nothing but it. Their sense of awareness must be very, very much more subtle and sensitive then the astute citizen prophet-sage and that places them in a very different category of being.

Their function is similar to the worm that eats only mulberry leaves and secretes an extremely exotic silken thread. (some say that when the cloak comes off there is resemblance)

Cosmic navigators however, subsist only on track of "Dark God encouragement" left to be found and assimilated and from it, they secrete a part of the exotic silken thread that forms overlapping perpendicular, vertically entangled, rotated and inverted stratum of Dark energy weft.

As incipient contributor to fabric of chaos they are aware of all nodal involution and differentiation in areas of familiar, foreign and unknowable energy potential in that boiling sea. Their pockets may be full of Dark salt as they slowly maneuver about the turbulent potentialities......... Why?

They are near membrane in order to direct "prendas" and deep in the untouchable vault of Dark chaos equity that maintains the storm momentum. ......Why?

They manage this by utilizing the same "key" that the citizen does. It is the only and ultimate key of access, ... soul,...... that is within both rationality and Dark chaos and is the vehicle/path of navigators.

When that special talent is available and "known" all navigators volunteer the sacrifice of non-participatory contribution. A refusal or option are not really considered as they have already realized their "type" of being.

With that surrender arrive "gifts" that even extreme prayer cannot provide. Gifts that the learned sage of the Fifth may only hold in dream. It is opportunity not for a selfish but a selfless reason, perhaps a gift of surrender to the higher purpose.

For example, ...when a spiritual potency called "Ntum" (by San people) releases the emerald fire experience, that rent in phenomenal membrane lays the Dark open for a micro-moment. (without Holy Trinity of creation) Like ancient San shamans,..... navigators climb into an available or predetermined? ....fractal tendril. They have the talent and use soul filament of Dark chaos in accessing servitude toward Godhead to conduct the business of chart mapping.

It is available because they perceive their form as that of an elongated moth-bird in flight and that can be used to spiral through those Dark tendrils avoiding inconceivable turbulence. Wiggling and squiggling silver threads of possibility will be identified before the sound of their cosmic background radiation can be heard,.....when they hover in the only place where fire can be lit more than once. (a Cave with no Name) A navigator is in fact a "type" of wiggling silver thread within reservoir sea. From that extreme chaotic position and due to an exotic kinship, possible directions of their cousin potentials can be mapped on an unrelenting "dynamic."

It is more "action" then sitting at an event horizon watching time come and go and therefore that much more rewarding.

Some unfortunate junior navigators are assigned rudimentary positions.

Then there is an example in the "Mantis God" navigator. When crawling about in rationality it will peek into dry, parched equilibrium with the idea of finding a snack on worldly debris of a slow ego based decomposition. (presence prayer) A presence of minimal contribution may be a "hollowness" of rational organic but the contribution of citizen may be its "wholeness." A tendril with direction allows raw energy of possibility to suggest definition in future perfect realm and if that direction can be mapped, manifestation may possibly be manipulated. (pre-determined)

That creative manifestation is the drop of moisture or sip brought out of a soul-well of access of Dark reservoir via a whirling spiral of chaos extrapolation that has been the vehicle/path of navigators. It is only a whirling spiral of "nothing but Dark," that every rational has assumed every rational has and in the presence of rational citizenry, it is identified as such. Of course "nothing but Dark, is potentially everything" and a whirling spiral carries about itself what is in proximity.

It requires a Mantis God navigator within a soul of pre-blossoming potential in presence, to bring the situation toward audition, for in that prior multitude are those that hold a hidden purity and grace.

A "Mantis God" navigator does not map Divinity or watch time come and go, it is the "cleaner" of rational debris and as such offers "absolution" to ego based decomposition in presence prayer to allow at least a neutral slate on which to build. Then under a "guidance" of audition dream created in those medieval towers, a maturing process facilitates climbing into the Fifth.

This method of positive growth is less obvious but is silent work of a water carrier that is continually necessary and an absolute fundamental in the formation of a civilization in house of best purpose.

(interesting that it arrive under a sign of Aquarius) These navigators are the most humble of the emerald green.

Same reward of extreme selfless contribution to energy gate of beautitude is the only recognition.

Other such "gifts" are also bestowed and their equal "other-worldliness" cannot be refused. Those with the talent live (in an emerald green aura) and contribute energy at an unbelievable rate. They are assured great embellishment of purpose in a "possibly" eternal non-identity realm.

Navigators direct prendas, (vessels of enlightenment) (occasionally in potentia) following those "ibal" (seeing instruments) outside of moment brevity without vision or audition prayer crowding simple "purpose" within filament "interval."

They may be "reading" other navigator directives as they themselves leave "print." (to be read) It is the mapping of a Divine dynamic "chart,".... clearing the way of phenomenal debris, ...or any of a multitude of other tasks,......yet almost always "choosing" or forwarding a will of Gods.

What interval can harbor this correspondence? It must occur in interval. Not the interval of light but what of an interval of Dark chaos turbulence?

Is there an interval anywhere/any-when within the Dark chaos energy reservoir of maelstrom? Yes,... it is an exotic emerald green aura that just barely glows as it circumambulates within a thread-like soul tendril. It will not "allow" energetic access or observation, (within aura) yet may, just as perpetuity principle describes, surrender to a subtle perturbation.

The faithful circumambulate the mystic Ka'ab searching for/finding "companion." It is heavenly witness and interpreter of the impenetrable. The navigator may tune the gong prayer of Ron's announcement of the Carpadian Fifth as "temple," perhaps suggesting/introducing rationality to soul "within," ....extrapolating from absolute "without."

The irritant that arrives may in part be due to motion of navigators themselves directing those fecund prenda toward a recipient "Cave with no Name" just before creation foundation. (Magik with one handful of fodder and one of energy possibility, anxious for applause)

Navigators may very well be involved in scope of perpetuity principle and that may be why their pockets are full of Dark Salt. They may be involved in the process of irritant.

(Why not consult fodder opinion in fecund opportunity. It may be quite valuable, and the necessary expendable ingredient that makes an energy contribution system "work," might, in the position of citizen actually have something to say.)

One might remember Nadia and Carpadia opening an emerald green portal that connected Holoflux with a quiet glen just outside the village of Schel's birth in the Carpathian mountains. It was initiated to beam a patient presence and invitation that would require a long Arctic journey.

The narrative of its occurrence described the interaction but did not mention how it was brought forth. Perhaps with a more acute knowledge of energy manipulation it may now be forwarded that Carpadia (savior of the Fifth) with help from Nadia and the coven of witches was coming into the "understanding of her "type" of being,"...... as a navigator.

She was learning how to move through soul tendrils of possibility chaos, to seed a manifestation of action that without e-mail required emerald green mail.

Carpadia was perhaps beginning to understand that she could follow track of God encouragement and as contributor to Dark energy weft could hold volition over some (as she was still quite young) incidence of manifesting phenomena.

A shaman's copper chest plate and thorn berry archway were the contraption that reflected the emerald portal. This was "method" of connection just as professor Who's "declaraphone" was, in the Horton story. Both were opening communication across vast distances and measures of scale.

This was possible due to navigation of potential prior to phenomenal limits.

"Key" understanding is endeavor of heart and soul.

Vlad's calming center after shaman rebirth into spirit, was displayed via copper chest plate.

Professor Who's contraption was display of "Who" civilization.

Cosmic assembly of star dust will be unashamed to display "yowa" of humankind.

In each case the "key" ingredient is/was a declaration of heart's desire. When effort passes beyond audition prayer and into visionary, a signal/beacon is presented that a navigator can focus upon to create direction, interaction and result.

A Qur'an, Caduceus, wand of Merlin, Speaker's staff, Cross or Tree glyph of a Qaballa may be beacon recognized as an aid to hero-navigators who would display "heart's desire" as a will of potential to "create" an imaginative phenomenal situation.

Three of the navigators of example circumstance are known, Carpadia, Mantis God and Horton and the next may be an "alternative" rational soul-bearing contributor.

Throughout "history" many navigators were known as "magi." They were Sufis, Tariqa and writers of "Upanishads." They were authors of "Yasna," true Zoroastrians and perhaps Neo-Platonics. They were of the "tribes of the Medes." They were Merlins of Malory, and developers of "gematria," Novikov and Schwarz of Russia and Crowleys and Schrodingers.

Without a beacon of signal, focus will be very difficult and navigators will simply go about the business of Divine mapping or service of clearing phenomenal debris, or whatever. If, however, they catch a marker, glimpsed in periphery of action along soul filament, perhaps a response just may be initiated. Directing a vehicle of enlightenment toward suspension of possibility may with a little salt, light a fire of auspicious opportunity,....... and worlds will open.

Manifestation only has position/situation when the total effect of interaction of intent is to generate the property of position, therefore creating a type of equity.

In a minor sense, it was emerald green e-mail and in a somewhat greater sense may be discovery of proximal civilizations. Beacon of the Fifth will burn brightly in Dark. It must display in confident patience. It is declaration of heart's desire "as a civilization," and will and must persist.

(or not) The Fifth civilization of humankind is aware of how and why rational organic has come into awareness and it will be in a house of best purpose.

As unique as navigators are, so are they the last bastion of anything conceivable at that already almost inconceivable scale of energy reciprocation before "End."

(the following is adaptation of Martin Heidegger's "History of Concept of Time" Trans. Theodore Kisiel, Indiana U. Press, 1985)

It is most simple of all and when that answer is made known it will be an end to these systems of contribution and perpetuity principle. Holy Trinity will be complete.

Completion is at a place of conclusion, it is at an end with nothing more outstanding. Process of creation has reached "wholeness," no more a process of purpose. Accordingly, as "full" not even the great creation possibility of Dark chaos sea can suggest a pre-possession.

From a point of view of physics, it is a situation when Dark salt can no longer come out of energy solution, perhaps due to dispersion. Without Dark matter irritant, perturbation theory as a pressure, gravity wave influence is defunct. Possible plural ones become the one wholeness of energy homeostasis with no dissolved crystalline instigators.

Creation suggests ownership yet could that which had opportunity to have been previously birthed from Dark chaos and Holy trinity possibly "be" at point brevity where "wholeness" has closed relic cosmological membrane?.....No. It is because of a basis, truth, or grace of its,..... "kind of being."

End of purpose cannot be "encountered" by creation principle. Dark storm and any activating ideas of potential have only ever had, on basis of true totality "possession of possibilities." Only method of and from awareness of such a basis, does possibility have potential ways to "be" in the first place. Participation is necessary for motion and when that is no longer offered and cannot be in confrontation it is "end."

That will relinquish fecund advantage and trigger and any "ownership" will also be forfeit. To imagine that such a cosmological creation scheme would desist must be an idea of always having "stood before." End of creation purpose "belongs" to Holy Trinity long before it becomes wholeness. It is not a hidden or ignored part but is ambiguous.

Yet why limit Dark chaos storm to a singularity? That is thinking like a rational organic, always wanting to "limit." Why would Dark storm not simply be just one of the ones. The spider's silken thread that contorts in vitality of mayhem until catching a fragile leaf on which to anchor and build may only be involved with one of unlimited possibilities of Dark storms. Each thread may be one of unnumbered filaments manipulated by this one chaos maelstrom.

If this Dark chaos realm is a divine principle of familiar rational organic there may or may not be other alternative soul bearing rationals worshipping and contributing to its embellishment. Perhaps each storm has only one familiar contributing element of awareness or maybe a family, nation, or civilization of contribution may worship the same Dark chaos creation sea.

Those, in very diverse situations may still be in a type of "resemblance" proximity.

If each singularity of creation scheme with its own Dark chaos reservoir was a "unit" contributor, then again, the Dark salt as irritant coming out of solution, pressure, gravity rent and point-creation, (the organics) of it could cease to be operational. It could be from any failure of the vulnerable balance of motion that occurs as the "above" of a rational organic's "below."

When in contribution "this" Dark creation chaos will have the identity just described but if embellishment ends all of its enhancement energy donation can no longer be "this" one.

Just as rationality stops contribution when organic ceases, so may it be a fundamental that Dark chaos energy storm may have to stop creation scheme contribution when "organics" of its system cannot continue. It is "end" in similar manner to the energy dispersion with no identity that is evident with familiar rational organic.

Creation scheme can no better be found in "wholeness" than identity can be found in Dark chaos reservoir. Although completely indefinite it is certain probability.

Printed in the United States
By Bookmasters